Where's Mom?

2004

Enjoy the trip as you travel through life!

Ricky Jensen

Where's Mom?

by Dicky Jensen

www.zamazamapress.com

2004

Dicky Jensen

ZamaZama Press
3109 Colby Avenue
Los Angeles, CA 90066
www.zamazamapress.com
Printed in the United States of America

Library of Congress Control Number: 2004111542.

ISBN: 0-9746714-1-X

First Edition
1 2 3 4 5 6 7 8 9

Editing and book design by Thema www.thema.us
Cover illustration and design by Maureen Burdock.

To my three great kids:
Kurt, Beth, and Ellen

Contents

Acknowledgement

To my youngest daughter, Ellen, who pored through many large cardboard boxes stuffed with diaries, letters, airplane ticket stubs, brochures, souvenirs, itineraries, and notes written on scraps of paper. Somehow she was able to make sense of it all. Thanks, Ellen, for the hours you spent bleary-eyed in front of the computer assembling and editing *Where's Mom*?

one

Death in Durham

During the past 18 years I have been a voluntary homeless person, traveling the globe. I have no job, no car, no house, no telephone number. All that I own can fit in a backpack and a box or two left at my daughters' homes. I got the last boat out of Haiti before the coup deposed Baby Doc Duvalier. I was in Germany when the Berlin Wall came down. I was in Hong Kong when it reverted to Chinese rule. When President Clinton visited Ireland, I was there. I had two audiences with Pope John Paul II. I went to the Olympics in Atlanta and Salt Lake City. I volunteered with the Israeli army and in a Palestinian village. I did a stint with the Peace Corps in the Czech Republic. I saw the terra cotta warriors in Xian, China, the Sydney Opera House in Australia, the *favelas* in Rio de Janeiro, and the Guggenheim Museum in Bilbao, Spain. I flew in a tiny mail plane beyond the Arctic Circle, and I dogsledded in Alaska. Did I mention that I am 78?

What made me decide to embark on this unusual lifestyle? My youngest daughter fired me. In 1984, two of my three children were launched, leaving only Ellen, a freshman at Brown University, still in the nest. When she came home for Christmas, the fireworks went off. I had foolishly thought that she would be happy to come back to Mother and our nice apartment on Main Street in Durham, N. H., a quaint college town. I envisioned us shopping, getting a bite to eat, and chatting about her first semester. But she had other plans. She was off skiing, meeting friends at the local watering holes, and talking on the phone. So when I asked her why she wasn't spending more time with me she looked at me as if to say, "Do you actually think I'm going to hang around with *you*? I have my own life to live and you're going to have to figure out how to live yours!"

Earthquake! The mother-daughter thing was over. For thirty years I had the job of wife, and I lost that one to divorce. Now my last child was out of my life, and I lost my job as mother.

Not everyone would take this fairly typical rejection as seriously as I did. After all, most people would say I was still sitting pretty. I had a comfortable apartment filled with the antiques I had collected during my marriage. I had friends. I had a respectable job working as a claims representative for Aetna Life & Casualty. I had just been promoted to senior claims rep. I had a company car.

But something crucial was missing.

For me, being a claims rep for Aetna had no meaning. Would I spend the next twenty years figuring out which car went through a red light or whether a client deserved $25,000 for his lower back pain? Would I spend my life sitting in this same apartment, looking at my antique spinning wheel and cradle?

Suddenly Aetna was just mammon; the apartment, a tomb. I knew my days in Durham were numbered and my budding career with Aetna was over. When Ellen insinuated, "Do you actually think I'm going to hang around with *you*?" she pushed me through the passageway.

By spring, I was out of there.

I sold my furniture. A friend in Massachusetts who had a small antique shop arrived with her pick-up truck and cleared my place out. What an exhilarating feeling as I watched the truck back out of the driveway loaded down with the dead wood.

I gave up my apartment. I wasn't going to live in it anymore so why pay rent on it? Why not put the money for the electricity bill, the heating bill, insurance, and garbage pick-up into something more alive?

I bought a backpack. I headed to Haiti.

 2

I believe I have found a unique way for a single, older person to have a vital, brilliant life. It's certainly not for everyone. But for me, living in an apartment by myself was akin to death. I had to find the strength and guts to break out of my routine of same job, same neighbors, same stores, same TV shows. Now the whole planet is my home. Every day is an adventure with new sights, new people, new foods, new beds, new cities, new diversions. I am out of the rut and alive.

two

Kill the Cat

When I told one woman about my lifestyle, she sighed and said, "Oh, I wish I could do what you do!"
"Why can't you?"
"I have a cat."
"Well, take your cat to the vet and have it put to sleep. Then you could do what I do."
"Oh!" in a shocked voice, "I could never do that!"
"Well, then you can't do what I do."

Okay, before the letters start coming from People for the Ethical Treatment of Animals, let me say that I am not actually advocating the killing of cats. What I am advocating is thinking creatively, breaking the barriers we hide behind. Did this woman really want her cat to determine how she was going to live for the next five or ten years? It's so easy to get comfortable in the cocoon we all build around ourselves. We hear the same political talk: Democrats are doing this and Republicans are doing that. But somewhere else in the world, people are talking about the Labor Party, the Likud Party, what Beijing is saying about Hong Kong's Rule of Law. We eat the same bran flake breakfast each morning. But somewhere in the world people start the day with rice and green vegetables. We shop at the same supermarket. But somewhere else in the world people are shopping at an outdoor market, going from stall to stall with a basket. We see the same mostly white faces every day and speak English with them in an American accent. But somewhere in the world people are speaking one of hundreds of different unfathomable languages.

So my point is that, with this one life we're given, why not make it as varied and exciting as possible? All it entails is hopping on a plane and landing in another country six or eight hours later and facing a whole new way of experiencing the world. Those barriers will come falling down.

We are very good at finding excuses for staying in that comfortable rut. Take money. People have the mistaken notion that you have to be very rich to travel. If you read travel magazines, the travel section in the Sunday newspapers, or the upper-class guidebooks, you can understand why people think this way. Hotel rooms are advertised at a "special price" of only $200 a night. So even though people are embarrassed, they still ask me, "Where do you get all the money to travel with?"

Nowhere is "outside of the box" thinking more apparent than in the economics of travel. I travel on my monthly Social Security check. My $1,160 check—the one that most people use to barely cover the cost of housing, car, insurance, television, and telephone—allows me to sail the seven seas, stand before the great pyramids of Egypt, explore Hong Kong, and walk the shores of Lake Louise in Canada.

So how do I do it?

I never take a taxi except in dire emergency. Taxi drivers are notorious for spotting a tourist and then ripping off said tourist. Every airport in the world has bus service. It takes a little longer to figure out how to reach my destination by bus, and I have to ask a few more questions, but I immediately begin to learn how to get around the city. I get a feel for its culture and its people. On the bus, I sightsee instead of nervously watching the taxi meter and wondering if I am being robbed.

I never eat in a restaurant where they have linen napkins and

 6

waiters. I can't afford it. Instead, I seek out cafeterias at universities; I buy salami and bread in an open market; and I find small diners. I also bring along a good can-opener and spoon. These items can be lifesavers when there's no cheap restaurant around. A can of spaghetti and sliced peaches off the grocery shelf, at fifty cents each, make for a nutritious, satisfying meal. Eating on a park bench while people-watching adds to the ambience. And I never despise fast-food restaurants. If I want an American style bathroom and a cup of coffee, there is no sight more welcome than the Golden Arches. I take it as a personal affront if anyone says something derogatory about McDonald's within earshot of me.

I visit tourist sights that don't charge admission. The way I look at a new town is that it contains about fifty sights worth seeing. Twenty-five of these places have an admission fee. The other twenty-five places are free. I don't have time to see all fifty so I see the free places. They're often better than the ones I would have to pay for. I go to libraries, museums, hotel lobbies, parks, the public streets, university campuses, lectures, and walking tours.

Now and then I have to break down and pay an admission fee for something extraordinary like a lecture by James Watson who discovered the double helix or a visit to Windsor Castle, but I spend much of my visits taking advantage of the freebies.

My biggest money saver of all is that I *never* stay in a hotel. For $15 a year, I am a member of the International Hostelling Association. This Association puts at my disposal 5,000 hostels all over the world for an average night's lodging of $15. Multiply that by thirty nights. That's $450 a month and it includes my heat, hot water, electricity, use of a kitchen, often a lovely breakfast, and a lounge with books and brochures. I don't have to worry about fire insurance, cleaning the gutters, shoveling snow, or making repairs. People say bad things about hostels. Ten years ago these bad things were true. The young folks were barefooted, had dreadlocks, and played their guitars till 3 a.m. The sheets were gray and conditions were primitive. Didn't anyone ever empty the trash? Hostels were open only to guests who arrived by foot or bicycle. You were expected to do chores. The hostels closed down in the middle of the day. Thank goodness, that's all changed now.

Hostels are one small step below a hotel. The International Hostelling Association sets high standards for safety and cleanliness; they even set the ratio of toilets to guests. Hostel staffs are trained to provide information on sightseeing and local events. The staff will make reservations for your next destination so you are assured a bed in the next city. It's called BABA: Book-A-Bed-Ahead!

When I described what a hostel was like to one of my friends, she asked, "You mean you sleep in the same room with strangers?" The word "strangers" had the same ring to it as "vampires" or "serial killers."

Yes, I do sleep in the same room with strangers, but for me the word "strangers" has the same ring as "new friends" and "interesting personalities." They are fellow travelers on the same journey that I'm on. They are usually young. They wear T-shirts and shorts to bed while I wear flowered pajamas. They hail from countries all around the Earth. They carry backpacks in a hundred different shapes and weights. They're pinching pennies. They're friendly. They're happy to share information.

Does that sound so bad?

Of course, there are a few down sides to hostel living, just like any experience in life.

The worst for me is the sound of zippers being opened and closed when I'm trying to sleep. It's like the sound of fingernails across a blackboard.

The second worst sound is the rattling of plastic bags. In the dead of night it sounds as loud as a brush fire.

I do have to bring my own towel and soap. There are no bellhops to carry my baggage, and I might have to walk down the hall to brush my teeth, take a shower, or use a toilet.

In 18 years of travel, I only asked to change my room once.

An obvious "bag-lady" lay on the upper bunk with a blank look on her face as she wrapped and unwrapped rubber bands around her fingers. The hostel staff understood immediately and transferred me to another room.

And the savings involved in hostelling are unbeatable. The hostel in Washington, D.C. costs $28 a night. It's two blocks from the Hyatt Regency Hotel where a room costs as much as $400 per night. While in DC, I walked to the Hyatt every morning for coffee and had the pleasure of sitting in the beautiful lobby and listening to the live piano player without the $400 price tag. The hostel in New York City is the biggest hostel in the world with 620 beds. It's immaculate and well run, and it offers free tours every day to the sights in the Big Apple. There's always a volunteer on duty in the lobby to answer questions about getting around in New York City. All this for $29 per night.

The hostel in Seoul, South Korea deserves special mention. When I got to the airport in Seoul, I took a taxi (circumstances required this small transgression) and asked the driver to take me to the youth hostel. He drove up the circular drive of a very imposing skyscraper hotel. I tapped him on the shoulder and gesticulated wildly, "No, no. This is hotel. I want *hostel*, hos-tel!" He went inside anyway and then waved me in. I stood on the marble floor of the sumptuous lobby and saw two distinguished men in navy-blue suits and white shirts standing very straight and proper behind the reception desk.

I said, "I'm sorry but I'm looking for the International Hostel."

"Madam, this is the International Hostel!"

I looked shocked and dazed, but the bellhop picked up my pathetic backpack, led me to the elevator, and accompanied me to the 11th floor. My room overlooked the distant mountains, the sky-line of Seoul, and Olympic Park. This was a regular commercial hotel but a few rooms had been set aside for hostelers. Each room had four beds, a shower and toilet, and a congenial table to sit at and

9

discuss travel plans. My roommates were from Japan, Singapore, and New Zealand.

That beautiful room with bath and shower cost me $8 a night just by flashing my International Youth Hostel membership card. No card—I would pay $86 a night! These accommodations were the most luxurious and cheapest of any hostel I have stayed in during my 18 years of travel.

I make it a point to stay only at official International Hostelling hostels. Sometimes an independent hostel is fine, but I am more likely to run into trouble.

I made a week's reservation at a hostel in Las Vegas thinking it was an official one because it named itself International Hostel. It was only $10.75 a night to be in Las Vegas. Perfect! As soon as I walked into the office, I knew I was in a dump. The manager had a beer belly, sheets were falling out of the shelves behind him, and the place was unkempt. I stayed my week and got around the discomfort by waking up at 7 a.m., making a beeline for the door, and visiting the beautiful Las Vegas hotels till ten at night. Then a quick shower behind the moldy shower curtain, into bed and oblivion. One night I found a note on the door, "Melinda – The police are looking for you." Later in the week one of my roommates decided she couldn't afford to keep her dog at the kennel any longer, so she brought her big, smelly Chow into our room to roam around all night.

Despite these bumps in the road, I can honestly say that the biggest plus of hostelling is the people I meet. Many folks, especially Asian travelers, are anxious to practice their English and that has led to many long, interesting conversations. In addition, I have made countless valuable connections for future trips by staying in hostels. How many times has someone said, "Dicky, when you are in my country, you must come and stay with me. I will show you ____ (fill in the blank)." And of course, when I am in that country, I accept these invitations.

Cheap traveling and staying in hostels go hand-in-hand. You

10

can't have one without the other.

Let me briefly recount two trips to illustrate these rules in action: one to Helsinki, Finland and one to Japan—both rumored to be very expensive. I had avoided them for a long time because of these rumors, but as I found out, you should not believe everything you hear. By traveling Dicky-style, I covered all of my expenses with my check from Uncle Sam.

In Helsinki, my hostel was in the heart of the city, a three minute walk from the train station. It cost $14 a night. There were eight beds in my room, but I was the only occupant. (Traveling in late September and October is perfect. There are no crowds and the weather is pleasant.)

For meals, I went to the university restaurant. I spoke to the Polish cashier and timidly asked, "May I buy coffee here?" as I was obviously neither a student nor Finnish.

"You can buy anysing you vant!" she said and immediately escorted me to the faculty dining room and said, "Eat."

A four-course meal, which included herring in cream sauce, a thick soup, borscht, baked fish stuffed with cheese and spinach, bread pudding, pancakes with jam, red and white cabbage salad, *Knackerbrot*, cost $4.50. I ate there every day and always said, "Sank you" to my new friend, the cashier.

Next, I took advantage of the free sights. Dominating the port of Helsinki is the gorgeous Lutheran Cathedral. Inside stand statues of Martin Luther and Melanchthon. That very evening a concert was given by the famous Boys' Choir of Atlanta, Georgia climaxing with a performance of Sibelius' *Finlandia*. Sibelius is Finland's most beloved composer and *Finlandia* is his most famous and emotionally-charged poem. The choir was fabulous! *Finlandia* expresses so much pride and patriotism that it became the anthem of the Finnish independence movement. What a way for a black choir from Atlanta to end its concert in Helsinki.

By the end of my visit to Finland, I had been to five free concerts, three church services, the herring market, the Opera House, two libraries, the City Theatre, the Sibelius Monument, and lots of hotel lobbies.

I figured out the costs for my thirteen days in Helsinki. Lodging was $182, food was $75, and I spent $64 in incidentals (tram tickets, postage, laundry, and second-hand winter hat and raincoat). It came to a total of $321 or $25 per day. At that time, I allowed myself to spend $31.50 per day from my Social Security. I was well within my budget.

The myth that Japan is prohibitively expensive (a cup of coffee in Tokyo costs $7, goes the myth) was quickly exploded my first morning in Tokyo. The tourist desk in Narita Airport arranged for the twenty-minute ride in the van from the Welcome Inn Hotel, a room, and a ride back to the airport the next morning—all for $42. I walked the neighborhood to see what I could find for breakfast and there I experienced the second explosion of the myth. I could have a healthy, satisfying breakfast for $2. That discovery was made in a convenience store like our 7-Elevens. A three-layer tuna, egg-salad, and cucumber sandwich, fresh and appetizing, cost $1.50. A hot can of coffee out of the vending machine cost 50 cents. I took both items outdoors, sat on a bench in the sun, and had my delicious breakfast as I watched the traffic and pedestrians go by.

For other meals these convenience stores came through with pizza, sushi, salads, and some unfathomable entrees that could be heated in their microwave —just like home! Another fun and cheap way to get a meal was to eat noodles or rice dishes in the train stations. These dishes cost from $2 to $4. I had to eat standing up, but after sitting on the train most of the day, that was no hardship. I certainly found the expensive things Japan is famous for—one apple for $10, a melon for $20—but I didn't buy them. I found the cheap things and bought those. I even found dollar stores. Except they're called Y100 stores. Y100 amounts to 83 cents in American money. There is the equivalent, too, of discount hair salons. I could get my hair cut in 10 minutes for Y1000 ($8). A note on the window said: "To Foreigners —You must bring along a person who speaks

Japanese or we will refuse to cut your hair." It made me wonder what kind of problems they had run into.

For sightseeing, I traveled on a 7-day rail pass that I bought in the US for $240. This rail pass was crucial because train travel in Japan is very, very expensive. One overnight trip can cost $200. But on my rail pass, I experienced the four islands that make up Japan: Hokkaido, to the north; the main island of Honshu; the smallest island, Shikoku; and the southernmost island, Kyushu. I viewed them from the comfort of an air-conditioned train, sitting in a cozy living-room-type chair. I went through the Japanese Alps, saw a sunset over the Sea of Japan, watched farmers at work in their apple orchards and rice paddies, saw typical Japanese homes with ornamental shrubs and landscaped gardens, and most thrilling of all, saw the majestic silhouette of Mt. Fuji, the most revered mountain in the world.

Many of the trains have only one car and one conductor. They go into the most rural areas, along rivers, and through mountain passes to accommodate the farmers who need transportation into town.

Each evening I stopped by the tourist desk in the train station and asked for help in finding a hotel room. This was an added challenge to keep costs down in Japan; in some of the out-of-the-way towns I visited, there were no hostels and I was forced to use hotels. But this challenge was met. The folks at the tourist desk helped me find a room usually no farther than two blocks away. I could stretch my arms out and touch each side of these rooms, but they had every amenity I could desire: a cotton bathrobe, slippers, a radio with wakeup alarm, soap, shampoo, a hair-dryer in the tiny bath, and a comfortable bed. The average price for a single room was $50.

The tourist desk was closed when I pulled into Kyoto. Panic time! Because until I have a room key in my hand, I am *nervous*! That is simply the way it is.

I had to walk through groups of young punks, guitar players, and scantily clad young girls with pierced belly-buttons and tattoos

13

(yes, our culture has arrived in Japan to their great loss). I saw a huge hotel a block away and figured I had no choice but to ask for a room there. Fully expecting to be ripped-off, I was relieved to be handed my key for a 12th-floor room with all amenities for $60. Challenge met again.

On another leg of my rail adventure, I met a friendly Japanese fellow, Kazuki, who struck up a conversation with me. He had lived in Vancouver, Canada for seven years and spoke beautiful English; I was very happy to allow him to be my new guide. He could read the complicated train schedules, knew how to get to the ferry which would sail to Beppu, Kyushu, and found a friendly restaurant where for $13 each we had a beer, beef and noodles, various kinds of pickles, and a pork cutlet on rice. At the convenience store he explained how sake, the famous Japanese rice wine, could be bought in all kinds of containers including what looked like a fruit juice carton. That size cost 90 cents. And Japan is prohibitively expensive?

So I travel on my Social Security checks. I see the world and I am forced to be creative about how I do it. Every day is an exciting experiment filled with new cities, new sights, and new strategies for keeping my budget low. I ignore those "special" vacation packages travel agents offer. My vacation packages are incomparable.

three

Look Before You Leap

ooking back, I almost cannot believe that I am still traveling given my very first trip. It was awful. Anxious to get out of my rut, I set myself a challenge way beyond what I was ready for.

I heard that the Episcopal Church needed volunteers in Port-au-Prince, Haiti. This seemed like useful work. I was not leaving my life in Durham on a whim but instead I was going to help my fellow man. And Haiti was only 400 miles off the coast of Florida so I would still be close to my beloved America. I called the sister in charge of the elementary school in Port-au-Prince who just happened to be visiting her diocese in Boston. I said I'd like to work in her school in Haiti. Could she use me? She immediately said yes. It was my first step to a new life.

I headed to Orlando, Florida to stay with my brother and study French, the official language of Haiti. My brother had a friend, a blind woman, who taught French, and I signed up for private lessons. Learning a new language is not one of my strengths so not too darn much happened with the blind lady.

After three months in Florida, I left for Haiti and my six-month commitment. I didn't fly in those days because of claustrophobia, so I had to get to Haiti on a cruise ship. I boarded a luxurious ship out of Miami that was going to make the rounds of various Caribbean ports. As my brother said good-bye to me, I thought,

"Oh, what am I doing on this ship going to Haiti? Have I completely lost my mind?" I was scared stiff. My brother comforted me saying, "There's no turning back. See you in six months—if you survive! Ha, ha."

Until we anchored at Cap-Haïtien, I indulged in all of the luxuries and endless food that only a cruise ship offers. I was, of course, the only one who got off the ship. Clutching my tiny backpack, I stepped from the luxury of a cruise ship into the chaos of Cap-Haïtien. Immediately I knew that although Haiti is only 400 miles from Florida, it is a world away.

Poor Haiti. Without a doubt it is the poorest and least developed country in the Americas. Its infant mortality rate is among the highest in the world. About four-fifths of the people cannot read or write. Because of poor diet and limited medical care, tetanus, tuberculosis, and malaria are common. The average Haitian lives only about fifty years.

But the worst problem in Haiti was its government. Francois Duvalier, known as Papa Doc, had himself elected president for life with the help of his goons, the Tontons Macoutes. These paramilitary brutes murdered anyone who disagreed with Papa Doc, and they put their decapitated heads up on poles for all to see. When Papa Doc died in 1971, his son Jean-Claude Duvalier, known as Baby Doc, took over as dictator. In 1986—while I was in Haiti—the people of Haiti rose up and Baby Doc and his spoiled wife, Michelle, were thrown out of the country and exiled to France.

The folks from the Episcopal Church said someone would meet me at the ship to drive me to Port-au-Prince. "Oh, no," the greenhorn confidently replied. "I'll get on one of those tap-taps." A tap-tap is a brightly painted minivan crammed with so many people that they hang out every window and ride on the roof. Thank God the sisters didn't listen to me because I would never have survived the ride.

I was driven to the big Episcopalian compound in the center of Port-au-Prince. My room had bars at all the windows—a bit unnerving. How would I get out in a fire? Who was going to try to get in?

But that was just the beginning of my fright. The whole Haitian atmosphere was scary. If I walked too close to the Presidential Palace, guarded by soldiers in khaki uniforms leaning on submachine guns, a whistle would blow and I was belligerently waved away.

Living in close quarters in the Episcopalian compound in Port-au-Prince, I heard all the daily gossip and happenings taking place in the city. I heard about the big thunderstorms which sent torrents of water rushing down the streets and down the unscreened drains. During one of these thunderstorms, four nurses were walking down the street arm in arm and the water pulled them down into the drain. A couple of days later their bodies were found out in the ocean.

Three hundred Mulatto families ran the entire country and owned most of its wealth. These Mulatto women shopped in Paris and sent their children to private schools in France. They rode around in chauffeur-driven limousines and had second and third homes in the cool mountains of Petionville. I heard that some of them actually bought fur coats in Paris and turned up the air-conditioning at their parties so they could wear their furs while they sipped cocktails

The six million other Haitians, their countrymen, lived in dirt floor huts and begged on the streets. There were piles of cement in the middle of the sidewalks, open man-holes, and children bathing in open sewers. One beggar woman outside our compound had a rope on her ankle which was tied to her little daughter. When the exhausted mother fell asleep, the daughter couldn't wander away. In the meantime, she was trying to sell three oranges.

While I was there the dictator, Baby Doc, and his wife, Michelle, drove through Port-au-Prince in a huge black stretch limo and threw money out the window. Their people were reduced to crawling around on the street hoping to snag a coin or two.

I was so mad. How dare these elite treat their own people so badly? Why was there so little value put on human life?

I went into complete shock. I kept wondering what had happened to my life.

At the beginning, my volunteer work consisted of making a valiant effort to learn Creole and updating the computer records of all the donors to the mission from around the world. The data entry was easy. I quickly realized that I wasn't going to learn Creole well enough to teach in a classroom. I was out of my depth. So I stalled. I worked very slowly so there would always be more updates to make. And I hoped against hope that I would never have to go into a classroom.

Finally, I got so scared that I became almost catatonic. I couldn't talk. I couldn't express myself. I knew I had to get out of there. I went to see Sister Teresa who I knew was very understanding. I had never been close friends with a nun before, but I quickly felt she was the epitome of what a sister would be like. Tall and slender with a gentle face, she walked through the hallways ever so quietly in her soft rustling robes, never in a hurry. I knew she would understand my problem and only have my well-being at heart. Somehow through my daze, I managed to tell her I was having a very hard time. She said, "You know, maybe you should think about going home." As soon as she said the word *home*, it all became crystal clear. That magic word *home*. "Yes, I want to go home. I have to go home." And that was it.

I immediately became energized and called my brother in Orlando. "Get me a reservation on the next cruise ship coming into Cap-Haïtien!"

Sister Teresa told me that one of her parishioners was driving up to Cap-Haïtien and I could go along with him to meet my ship. He was taking a mattress to a family up there. The mattress was tied to the roof of the car with kite string. About two hours into our trip, he noticed that the mattress had blown away.

I had been sitting on the edge of my seat wishing us in

Cap-Haïtien so I could get on that cruise ship and home. Now we had to drive back, away from my ship, and search for the mattress. He stopped at the various police stations along the way asking if someone had turned in a mattress. My path to freedom was disappearing. "Please God," I prayed. "Find us the mattress!" Finally at the fourth police station, we got the good news that the mattress had been turned in. The man retied the mattress with his kite string, and we were once again headed north to the coast.

When I saw the cruise ship anchored in the harbor, gleaming white in the sunlight, it was the most beautiful sight I had ever seen. I was rescued.

The driver drove right up to the gangway. When he stopped, a beggar woman appeared at my car window with a tiny baby in her arms. She shouted at me, "Money—money—baby (pointing to the bundle in her arms)—baby."

I shouted back, "I have three babies. I keep my money for my babies. Big deal, you have a baby. I raised mine. Go raise your own baby." I was obviously not rational.

I went up the gangway and on to the deck where there was an outdoor bar. I went straight to it, sat on a stool, and said, "Budweiser." I never sit on bar stools because I don't feel it's a woman's place, but like I said, I wasn't functioning normally. I drank three cans of beer right in a row and felt wonderful, if a bit woozy.

As it turned out, the government refused to let any more cruise ships dock and this was the last boat out of Haiti. Since I could not fly because of my claustrophobia, I would have been trapped in Haiti forever!

Then, of course, the ship had to finish its tour to St. Thomas and St. John, but I wasn't interested in these sights. I just wanted to get home. We finally got back to Miami and I hopped a bus for Orlando. When I walked into my brother's condo, I could feel myself being slowly put back together again. I was back in my own culture.

On my first trip, I had made a mistake going to the poorest

19

country in this hemisphere. But I still knew that I would never go back to a job or an apartment or my dead antiques. There would be a next trip, but it would be someplace that felt more familiar.

Soon a new idea began to form in my mind. My grandparents emigrated from Germany, so I grew up eating *Kartoffelsalat* and *Bratwurst*. I spoke only German until I was five years old. In a few weeks, I was planning my trip to Marburg, Germany, where I hoped I would feel more comfortable.

four

Why Don't You Act Like I Do?

hen I think back on my time in Haiti, my mistake
is clear. I had acute culture shock. In Marburg, I
hoped my German background would eliminate
the alienating elements of culture shock while I
still embraced the adventure of a different way of life. And yet,
while I can rationally explain what happened and what still happens
in a new place, I can't stop the effects of culture shock. No matter
how long I travel, I still have moments of irrational panic upon
arriving in a new country. One panic attack occurred in 1999 after I
had been on the road for 13 years. Why did it happen? The only
explanation I can offer is culture shock.

I was on a bus from Bilbao, Spain, to Frankfurt, Germany. I
had a captivating time in Bilbao staring for hours at the new
Guggenheim museum, taking in the sights, touring the La Rioja
wine district of Spain. I looked back to Spain with complete satisfaction. But then I looked ahead to Germany. I had been there at
least five times before, including a year and a half living and teaching in Butzbach, a town outside of Frankfurt. I spoke solid German.
I loved the food, was familiar with the money, and planned to visit
many old friends. I should have been at ease, but instead, I was pan-
icking.

I began to worry about not having any Deutschmarks when I
arrived in Germany. What if the ATM machine didn't work? What

if I couldn't find a place to sleep? My confidence disappeared. Why was I on this silly trip? Why didn't I stay home where life was simpler?

Of course, it was all nonsense. The ATM machine in the huge Frankfurt train station spit out 400 Deutschmarks with no problem. (I immediately treated myself to a bratwurst smothered in mustard.) The efficient tourist office explained exactly how to get to the big, well-run hostel, which had plenty of rooms and sat right on the bank of the Main River. The Three Kings Cathedral was two blocks down the street. The Römer Platz, home to city hall, the Christmas Market, the Catholic cathedral, and a huge Christmas tree were right across the river. I simply had to walk across the bridge and I was in the heart of Frankfurt.

So why was I apprehensive? It was the transition between cultures. I had adjusted to Spanish and pesetas and wine for lunch; now I had to think in German, use Deutschmarks, and start drinking beer. I know now that sometimes when I travel my mind plays tricks on me. All I can do is forge ahead and wait for the bad feelings to go away. And they always do.

I had a similar experience in Hong Kong, a city in a class by itself. It swarms with life, and it can be overwhelming. I have come to love Hong Kong, but my first visit there started out as a major fiasco. In my guidebook, I found the Victoria Hostel which sounded proper and British—just my type. But when I asked the taxi driver to take me there, he turned down a narrow, littered street teeming with people. Neon lights flashed everywhere and loud music blared. "Oh, please, don't let him stop on this street," I said to myself, as the taxi came to a halt. He stopped in front of a tiny opening between two stores. Above the opening was a tiny sign: Victoria Hostel.

I made my way up the dark, narrow stairway to the second floor where I was met by the Indian desk clerk. "Yes, let me show you the room." Up two more flights and then he opened a door onto a most unthinkable scene. The room was tiny with no window and

22

one dim light bulb. Eight metal bunk beds were jammed into the room, each bed with a flimsy, dirty curtain drawn across it. Four of the curtains moved. Without a sound, slanted, frightened eyes peered out above the curtains to see who had just opened the door. These were not tourists.

Culture shock! Scenes of prisons, the Death March of Bataan, and solitary confinement flashed across my mind.

I looked at the desk clerk with horror on my face and said, "I can't stay here."

"I have another hotel across the street. I will show you."

We left the concentration camp and headed across the crowded street. In front of this "hotel" stood a prostitute trying to lure men downstairs to a dance hall. The Indian led me into an ancient elevator the size of four telephone books. I held my breath as he took me to the room. Well, it had a window. The light was a little brighter. However, one of the guests in this room was a man, which did not add to my peace of mind. But by now it was four o'clock in the morning, my time, and I was reeling with fatigue. I had no choice but to stay.

My brain was already hard at work planning my escape back to America tomorrow.

There was no way I could stay in such filth, disorder, and noise. It didn't matter what it would cost me to change my plane ticket. I was going home, and the sooner the better.

The next morning was Sunday, and the street was quiet. Two old Chinese women were sweeping the pavement and bundling up cardboard to sell. I thought, well, I'll just have breakfast before returning to the airport.

I asked a passerby, "Where is McDonald's?" When I'm in a McDonald's I feel like I'm home. McDonald's is America.

She gave me simple directions. Maybe my luck was changing. Soon I was in McDonald's with all the familiar pictures and menus. After a cup of coffee and a stack of pancakes, the world began to look better.

Maybe I should do a little exploring before I go to the airport, I thought.

Within minutes I was at the famous Hong Kong harbor which was filled with every conceivable boat: junks, fishing vessels, ferries, yachts, tour boats, and fire and police boats. There across the harbor was Victoria Peak and gleaming glass skyscrapers.

Maybe I should stay on for a few days as long as I'm here, I said to myself.

I found a better hostel and moved out of the Victoria. I got used to the litter, the endless people, the lights, and the noise. I stayed on for four weeks and have been back three times since. In short, I came to love Hong Kong with a passion.

This scene has repeated itself many times. I go to sleep sure that I will be on a plane the next day, only to wake with a new attitude, ready for more adventure.

My biggest challenge in terms of culture shock was China. I never travel with a tour group. I don't like to conform to other people's schedules; I want to see more than the sights dubbed worthy by the tour company; and I don't like paying an arm and a leg for my travel. But I may have been better off in China on a tour.

When I arrived in Beijing, I thought I was on another planet. Thousands of bicycles crowded the roads carrying everything from live ducks to TVs. People wore face masks to protect themselves from the rampant pollution. New construction was everywhere as the old China was bulldozed away to make room for new shopping malls and glass hotels.

My guidebook had information on a small hotel which had a hostel in the basement where I could stay for $10 per night. That's where I wanted to go.

There was no official tourist bureau at the Beijing train station so I had to rely on hustlers who were advertising taxis into town. I generally take the bus, using taxis when there is no other choice. For me, there was no other choice in Beijing.

A young hustler led me out to the parking lot where a small

black car waited. The driver didn't know a word of English.

Yes, I was scared.

I refused to get in the cab.

"Why don't you get in the cab? Driver is very good," said the hustler.

"Because I don't believe that he will find my small hotel. I can't talk to him and he can't talk to me. I will be completely lost in a city of 12 million. I won't get in the cab unless you go along so I have somebody who speaks English."

He knew he was overcharging me by at least four times and didn't want to lose this sucker so reluctantly he got in.

And a good thing, too. The small hotel was down a *hutong*, or alleyway, which was indistinguishable from thousands of other alleyways. The hustler had to stop to ask directions at least seven times. Finally he located the narrow, bustling *hutong* and the Lu Song Yuan Hotel.

The second confrontation took place with the hotel clerk. No, there is no hostel here, she told me. We only have rooms for $50 each night.

"No, there is a hostel here and I want a bed for $10. Get the manager. Look here in my guide book."

Much discussion.

"All right, you can have the bed for $10. It's downstairs."

Exactly. Just like the book said.

This was a foretaste of how life is conducted in China, the most challenging country I have ever traveled in.

It sounds simplistic, but while traveling in China I had to remind myself that I was in a different culture, that I couldn't use my own culture as a measuring stick. My body, my psyche, and my brain were used to seeing things done one way. Suddenly I was in a country where things were vastly different. And no matter how often I told myself not to judge Chinese culture negatively because it differed from my own, I did it anyway.

Take the matter of spitting. After three trips to China, I still can't tolerate spitting no matter how often I give myself this lecture: "This is their culture. This is what they do. Don't get angry about it. Don't give people dirty looks when they spit. This is China. This is not America."

Was I ever able to accept this cultural difference? No. Instead I learned how set in cement cultural traits are. I understood better why wars are fought, why people hate each other, why some differences can never be resolved. We are prisoners of our own culture. This was a shocking discovery.

That's why traveling in Canada or England is stress free. These people are like me. They speak my language, they observe the same rules of etiquette, and they have the same outlook on life. But in China I was not comfortable. Chinese values are not my values. I reacted with nervousness and sometimes with downright antagonism.

"Why are they spitting? We don't do that WHERE I COME FROM!"

"How dare people talk out loud during a concert with no regard for the people giving the concert? We would never do that WHERE I COME FROM!"

"And why don't the people trying to get on a bus wait till the people are off the bus before pushing their way on? We don't do that WHERE I COME FROM!"

And on and on: "You don't cover your head with a scarf?" "You pray to that statue?" "You speak a different language?"

That's why so many people prefer to go on organized tours when traveling to foreign countries. It's a protection people need in order not to be exposed to too many cultural differences at one time.

And usually, I think this exposure to cultural differences is the big pay-off in traveling. I have to leave my comfort zone. My predictable lifestyle is gone. I am forced to see how other people live their lives and reassess why I live mine the way I do. My world is knocked cock-eyed! When this happens, I know my trip was worthwhile.

But China pushed me to the limit.

You miss so much if you go on a tour, I reminded myself. Yes, you see buildings and artwork and scenery, but you don't see the people. Hadn't I just experienced this vividly in front of the Art Gallery in Beijing? I was watching old men and children flying kites. A tour group came out of the Art Gallery and went straight into their air-conditioned bus and drove off. The most fascinating aspects of Chinese life were right in front of the tour group but they were already on their way to their Western style hotel. There they would be bowed to by beautiful, slim Chinese women wearing long, exotic Mandarin dresses. There would be the usual bars, fitness rooms, soft Western music in the background—everything they had at home. They wouldn't have to figure out the menu. It would be set before them in lacquer bowls and exquisite porcelain. That afternoon they would be driven to a temple, a shop where the prices are quadrupled, maybe another museum.

In the meantime, since I was on my own, I could leisurely watch people launch their brilliantly shaped kites. I could watch the short, toothless man who flew his kite the highest. I could get a close look at the heavy, specialized spools for winding and rewinding the nylon thread. And I could watch the exhilaration of kiteflying for as long as I wanted to because I had no schedule.

Having absorbed this fascinating scene, I walked a little farther into the park where women barbers, dressed in white coats, had set up shop. They brought chairs from home and were charging the equivalent of three cents a haircut. Several tried to entice me to have a haircut. It was great fun bantering back and forth. The people on that tour missed real life in China as they sat in their buses and chatted with their friends from New Jersey and Chicago.

So I did China without tours and I saw the "real" China. It was hard. I came back angry and disillusioned and vowed never to return. I forgot my vow and did return to give it another try. Again I went back to the US really angry and disillusioned, with another vow never to return. But there's something about China that gets in your blood. Not smart enough to know when to stop banging my head against the wall, I went back for a third time, throwing myself again into the cultural divide. But I never really got over my culture shock.

Someone once said that the two marks of a civilization are how you shit and how you eat. In my arrogant Western opinion, the Chinese flunk on both counts.

While visiting an Academy of Fine Arts, I ate in a student restaurant twice a day. The students and professors threw their napkins on the floor along with their cigarettes. They spit various bones and gristle on the table. Their heads disappeared into their enamel bowls and great slurping sounds emerged. Both arms rested on the table as they shoveled food into their mouths. I couldn't reconcile the fact that these were students and professors of the fine arts.

In Changsha, I met a Chinese-American woman, Dr. Mei Lu. She had lived in America for thirty-five years teaching neurobiology at the University of Chicago, Northwestern, and Brown. She owned a home on Cape Cod. The ancestral tug brought her back to Changsha because her father and grandfather were born there. She felt she owed the country of her birth a debt and wanted to repay this debt by teaching for three years at the Hunan Medical University in Changsha. But even she didn't count on the culture shock.

Her first obstacle was the condition of the bathroom in the building where she taught. She went to the head of her department and told him that it would be impossible for her to work unless something was done about the unspeakable condition of the bathroom. He said that nothing could be done and it would stay as is. Period. She could not accept this. She hired some peasants from the outskirts of Changsha at her own expense, bought the proper cleaning materials, and showed them how she wanted the entire bathroom scrubbed from the ceiling down. When it was cleaned to her satisfaction, she bought a lock for the door so no one could befoul it.

Her second obstacle was the apartment she was assigned to on the fifth floor of a faculty housing complex. She approached the other professors' families who shared this building to ask them to form a working committee so that the dirty, dark staircases and hallways could be cleaned up and whitewashed. They were strewn with melon rinds and potato peelings and the walls were black with grime. The families she spoke to couldn't comprehend what she was talking about. The staircases had nothing to do with them. Why would they possibly want to clean them up?

She was well into her first year when we met, and she didn't know if she could fulfill the obligation she felt. And she was Chinese.

The cultural differences go beyond mere cleanliness. I asked a receptionist in Hangzhou where the McDonald's was. She gave me very clear directions. I set out the next morning to find my stack of pancakes and American coffee. I walked up and down the street she had directed me to, checking side streets, frantically searching for the Golden Arches. They were not there. Later she admitted that her city had no McDonald's, but she didn't want to be the bearer of such bad news so she made up an imaginary McDonald's.

I asked another young woman at a bus stop how to get to Cheung University. I showed her where it was on the map. Yes, she understood my question. She told me to get on the #30 bus with her, stay on till the end of the line, and there I would find the university. Instead I found myself on the outskirts of town; the university was in a completely different direction. But she felt obliged to answer my question even though the answer was wrong. No wonder I felt schizophrenic in this country.

And try to buy a train ticket! This simple task can consume half a day. I needed to buy a ticket from Changsha to Beijing and I had my nephew, John, with me who speaks Chinese. Now how did this white kid from a typical white family, school, and neighborhood outside L.A. end up in China with an ability to converse in Chinese? Why do some people become chefs or accountants or you name it? The sing-song quality of the Chinese language and the intricate Chinese characters intrigued him. Although I secretly felt that it was the Chinese women who intrigued him, I'm still waiting for a wedding invitation.

To communicate with the ticket agent we had to bend down to a tiny window about six inches in height. The rest of the window was covered with metal bars, exactly like a prison. A tank couldn't get through.

What are they afraid of? I thought. Simple peasants, business men, and a few brave tourists simply buying a train ticket from Point A to Point B. Why make such a big deal out of it?

When John explained in Chinese that we wanted to buy a ticket to Beijing for a date three days from now, the ticket agent waved us away with his hand and yelled, "Tomorrow." He began to help the next customer.

John persevered. "No, we don't want to come back tomorrow. We want to buy our ticket today."

Again the hand waved us away, "Tomorrow!"

Frustration! Culture shock!

The next day we went through the same procedure: taxi to the train station; wait in a long line; bend down to the tiny window; make the request for a ticket. For some unfathomable reason this was the right day and I got my ticket.

The Academy of Fine Arts in Hangzhou was another lesson in culture shock. In the guest house where I stayed, the laundry was strung out over the stairwell. Sheets were drying over the banisters. Each of the four academy buildings had glass cabinets lining the halls for the purpose, I could only deduce, of exhibiting the students' work. These cabinets were all bare and filthy. The walls and floors were grimy. The rooms were dark and depressing. In one room I spotted two empty iron beds. They had no mattresses or bedding, just the exposed metal springs. Behind a dirty window pane was an excellent old Chinese painting. I asked about the beds. I was told two students had to sleep there every night to guard the painting from thieves. It was the antithesis of what you'd expect in an academy of fine arts, at least from my Western point of view.

It's safe to say that every country has its rip-off artists when it comes to tourists. The tourists are unfamiliar with the money, often flustered, and in a hurry. They are the perfect target. China brought this "art" to a new level.

I picked out a lovely quilt at a market near the Ming Tombs. The Chinese couple who sold me the quilt was so friendly. They smiled constantly. When I left with the quilt in an opaque plastic bag, the husband and wife waved, "Sank you, lady! Bye, lady. Sank you, sank you, lady!" I felt good about the quilt I had purchased and the friendliness of the Chinese couple.

Until I got back to my hotel, worked my way through the five knots in the bag and found a quilt smaller in size, uglier, and shop-worn. Why hadn't I paid better attention and checked the contents of my bag before I left the market? Because, frankly, I don't think that way. I expect to be treated fairly and honestly. It was the clash of cultures once again.

But the biggest rip-off happened with my friend, Alice Lau, an English teacher I met in Changsha. She was a delightful young Chinese woman, beautiful, hard-working, ambitious, and fun to be with. I asked her if she would like to accompany me to Xian, a must-see sight in China where the 6,000 terra cotta warriors have been excavated. It's the greatest archeological find of the century. If she would handle buying the train tickets and finding our hotels and restaurants, I would assume all expenses. It sounded like a fair trade for both of us.

The rip-off began when Alice began talking about bringing her sister along, clearly assuming that I would pay for her, too. I had never met the sister and didn't want to finance an eight-day vacation for her. Alice's reasoning was, "But we are sisters and like to be together." So? This was going to be a lesson in Chinese Thinking 101.

The second lesson in Chinese thinking occurred the day we

were to leave on our trip to Xian. The sisters said they would meet me at nine o'clock, but arrived at eleven o'clock. They said it was due to heavy traffic. They were both wearing brand new, sparkling white running shoes so I knew they had spent the morning shopping. But why did they have to lie about it?

The lies continued. They were supposed to meet me at a restaurant but they never showed up because they "had a problem with their camera and had to get it repaired." Later they happened to mention that actually they were with friends at the Big Goose Pagoda Restaurant.

Then there was the telephone call to my hotel from Alice saying she would be two hours late for another dinner date because she was at a calligraphy exhibition and "Chinese love calligraphy and I want to enjoy it. But Chinese don't like to rush so I have to take my time to enjoy it. But we'll be there in an hour and have dinner together so don't eat anything." I immediately ate a bowl of noodles. I was finally catching on to how Alice worked. The next call came: "We are at a hotel with friends we ran into from Changsha. If you want to join us I'll come to the hotel to get you." Another lie. This meeting with friends was planned all along. I was being used as a sucker, a cheap way for Alice and her sister to see the sights while I paid the bills.

I was fit to be tied. When Alice showed up I let her have it with both barrels. I called her a liar, a betrayer, told her she was using me. Why the secret about meeting her friends? It's one lie after another. I was so mad I had to stand out on the street for an hour to cool off. I decided then and there I had to get back to the good old USA and leave this convoluted society behind.

When Alice got back to our hotel at 11 o'clock that night and I had cooled down, we talked for two hours to figure out what made this trip go so wrong. Our conclusion:

She lives in one culture and thinks a certain way.

I live in a different culture and think a certain way.

And never the twain shall meet.

She thought she was comforting me with those lies, but they only incensed me because I knew they were lies. She didn't see it that way. Of course not. Her thinking is different from mine.

I did try one more time to recoup my dignity. I told Alice that she and her sister would have to pay for the sister's share of the trip. Clearly they had more money than I did, I argued.

Dicky: "On the first day of our trip you bought a $45 camera and lots of film. I can't afford that kind of a purchase."

Alice: "But this is an investment for the family. They have to have memories of this trip."

Dicky: "You and your sister have way more clothes than I have. You wear a different outfit every day. I've been wearing the same slacks since I left Los Angeles six weeks ago."

Alice: "But our clothes are very cheap."

Dicky: "You are constantly buying things like souvenirs, walnuts, ice cream, toys, a baseball cap, jewelry, three big melons, and other fruit that have to be dragged home on the train."

Alice: "But these are gifts for our family. We must do this."

The bottom line: They said they didn't have the money to reimburse me for the sister's part of the trip.

Foreigners in China have a saying for these types of experiences: T. I. C. "This is China."

I met Tom, an executive with an American company who told me that he has worked in China for 15 years and he still gets angry every day. When I told him some of my frustrations he said, "T.I.C." When Alice, her sister and I got back to Changsha, I took the first train out for beautiful, civilized, *British* Hong Kong. When I got there a typhoon was raging.

It was the most beautiful sight I had seen in my life.

All of which begs the question. Why did I go back to China three times? Despite this litany of complaints, China is fascinating. I met some wonderful people. There was Mr. Yu Anfei of Hangzhou who patiently tried to answer my questions about the Chinese. "Why don't the students at the Academy of Fine Arts speak to me?"

I felt I acted openly and friendly and smiled a lot to invite conversation, but they pretty much looked the other way.

"There are three reasons," he replied. "They think their English is too poor. They are still nervous that if they are seen talking to a stranger, it will go into their files and will jeopardize their chances for a future job. Finally, the academy is a relatively small school—750 students—so it is more provincial."

I also asked Mr. Anfei about his experiences during the Cultural Revolution, a question I had been dying to ask. He answered: "It was a very bad experience. We were forced to eat leaves, roots, and bark. Most of my classmates and I suffered from dropsy. This sickness causes swelling of the eyes and face. My stomach bothered me for the next ten years and I had to be hospitalized often. We were sent out into the woods in organized groups to pick leaves and bark and bring them back for the cooks. Most of the people who died during this time were those who had led a decent life. They didn't have the coping skills to survive. The poor fared better because they had always coped with bad conditions."

Another warm, generous Chinese man I met was the director of sculpture at the Academy of Fine Arts who had me over for a "humble" meal of lima bean and bamboo-shoot salad; two kinds of dried tofu; a special shrimp which only lives in West Lake at Hangzhou; a pork dish; a soup containing four fruits; pink, sticky rice shaped into a flower and filled with bean curd; a green vegetable I had never seen before; and two types of dumplings.

I also met Mr. Chen-Shiang Tang, 81, and his fiancé, 75. While strolling around beautiful West Lake in Hangzhou, I happened to make eye contact with this older couple sitting on a bench enjoying the sun. They gave me a tentative smile. I said hello. They made room for me on their bench which meant we were now free to converse. I asked the gentleman if he had ever been to America. He said, to my complete astonishment, "Yes, I studied at Washington University in St. Louis in the post-graduate school." My alma mater! He couldn't believe that I, too, had graduated from

34

Washington University. A very animated and exciting discussion followed. "Do you remember Forest Park? Kiel Auditorium? Dr. Arthur Holly Compton, our Chancellor? Exhausted, we capped off our visit having lunch at Kentucky Fried Chicken. At Mr. Tang's request, I wrote a letter to Washington University asking that he be sent a copy of his graduation certificate since he had lost all his documents during the Cultural Revolution. I enclosed a picture of the two of us Wash. U. alumni, standing in front of Hangzhou's famous pagoda.

I loved China also for the sights I saw. I saw pagodas with interesting names like Releasing Crane and The Peak that Flew From Afar. I saw the Forbidden City, Mao's birthplace, Tianamen Square, temples, the beautiful West Lake with boats in the shape of dragons and temples, the Great Wall, the Ming Tombs, the body of Mao Tse-tung. I waited at bus stops and watched the hundreds of bicycles going by carrying farmers with their vegetables and crates of screaming ducks and chickens, women immaculately dressed in Western style suits with stockings and high-heels, and entire families perched on the front and back tires. An endless, fascinating parade.

Perhaps I went back to China to get a handle on Chinese thinking or maybe to beat their system. But it's 1.2 billion to one— rather formidable odds. And maybe I went back to China because the vast culture gap made me think on my feet, kept me razor-sharp and wide awake. And isn't that why I travel?

five

Taking Advantage of Friends and Relatives: United States

There are times when even I need a break from my peripatetic lifestyle, when I want to wake up in the morning and not have to think about how I am going to find breakfast or where I will sleep that night. I remember being in Oslo, Norway, finishing up a tour of Sweden, Denmark, Poland, and Finland. The cities I visited were beginning to run together, and I was beat. The human body and brain can only absorb so much and then they need a rest. I needed a rest in suburban America. I wanted to go to the grocery store, vacuum the living room, and watch Larry King. As I have no home to return to, I head to the homes of my relatives.

I have spent hundreds of free nights in lovely homes in fascinating cities simply by calling on my brothers and sisters, my nieces and nephews, my children and friends. They are paying the mortgage and keeping up the repairs on their homes, and I am staying for free. Am I an inveterate free-loader? No. I never stay any place without offering a service in return—usually manual labor. By the time my one-week or two-week visit is over, my friends and relatives are thanking *me* for coming to their house.

My brother Fred and his wife Marilyn are always happy to have me live in their home in Los Angeles when they leave for a few weeks to visit their kids. I have a two-story house to roam around in, a 36-inch TV, the *Los Angeles Times* delivered to my front steps each morning, lots of food in the refrigerator, and the use of a Honda Civic.

What service do I provide in return for this life of luxury? I scour the refrigerator, clean and reorganize all the drawers, water hundreds of flowers. One year, I stained the deck and replaced the rotten floorboards. This is not drudgery because I do it so seldom. It's actually kind of fun to pretend to be a home-owner when you have none of the real responsibilities.

When I've done a few hours work, I take advantage of the city around me, in this case, LA. I visit the Getty Museum, poke around the UCLA campus, visit the interesting towns of Westwood and Santa Monica, and drive through Hollywood and Beverly Hills.

My brother and sister-in-law return, and their house is spotless, the garden is thriving, tasteful flower arrangements are placed here and there, and dinner is waiting for them. In addition, their home has not been broken into. "Oh, Dicky! Thank you so much! Come back anytime!" they say.

Thank you, I will.

My brother Charlie has a lovely home in New Smyrna Beach, Florida. He loves to travel, too, so when he is off seeing the world, I'm on my hands and knees in the hot Florida sunshine picking caterpillars off his oleander bushes, fighting red ants as I weed the garden, watering, watering, watering, and cleaning, cleaning, cleaning. But who's complaining? I have the Atlantic Ocean at my doorstep, miles of beach to walk along, and a comfortable air-conditioned house I can call my own for a few weeks.

Through Charlie I also landed a two-week stay in New York City as a cat-sitter. His friend, Carol, wanted to go on a cruise, but needed someone to look after her cat and her apartment in Beekman Place, a ritzy apartment complex near the UN. Would I do it? She didn't need to ask twice.

Her apartment came equipped with a doorman who extended a friendly welcome every time I entered the building and said goodbye every time I left; an elevator man who always knew my apartment was on the fourth floor; a view of the New York skyscrapers you wouldn't find in many five-star hotels.

I called my nephew who works for Fox Studio in California and asked him if he had any good ideas of unusual things I could do in New York. He's a first-class networker so I knew he'd come up with something. Sure enough, he sent me to the New York Stock Exchange and told me to ask for Louise Jones who he promised would get me onto the floor of the Exchange. When I arrived, the security guard found Louise and she ushered me right on to the floor of the Exchange. She instructed me to follow her around as she was very busy watching TV monitors, jotting down numbers on slips of paper, responding to requests to buy or sell. I couldn't believe my good luck. I had entered a world very few people enter. She ordered out sandwiches for both of us. While gulping one down, she told me she was one of thirty women who has a seat on the Stock Exchange out of a total of 1366 people. She manages sixty people and has been doing this job for eighteen years. She pays $6,000 a month rent for her apartment in Tribeca, $700 a month to park her car and $3,000 a month for a weekend place in Rockland, NY. But now, she said, she would like to step off the roller-coaster, have a baby and a different kind of a life. She started by giving up coffee six weeks ago and had a major headache for three weeks.

My two weeks in New York also included attending two standing-room-only plays, *Fosse* and *Aida*; walking the six blocks down to NBC to watch Katie Couric and Matt Lauer work their magic on the *Today Show*; attending a Jewish rally and a Palestinian counter-rally on 2nd Avenue; hanging around to watch President Clinton's motorcade go by as he took Hillary to the Four Seasons for her 53rd birthday; stopping in at a Christie's Auction (no admission fee) to watch the rich and famous of New York bid on the de Portanova Collection of jewelry; watching people in the 8th floor lobby of the Marriott Marquis at Times Square; eating at Katz's Delicatessen on the Lower East Side which became famous during World War II with its slogan, "Senda Salami to Your Boy in de Army."

Two weeks in New York City in a free apartment is a gift from the gods. When my time was up I kissed Carol's cat, said good-bye to the elevator man, and good-bye to the doorman. And Carol returned to her clean apartment and happy cat.

My sister Beba's ranch and winery in Redwood Valley, California, is another favorite stopping place for me. She is the proprietor of the Frey Winery which produces many varieties of organic wine. Everyone is drinking it now because it doesn't give you a headache. The Frey Ranch sits on 450 acres of land, mostly vineyards and groves of redwoods. When they bought it thirty years ago it cost $25,000. It's now worth several million. Do I take advantage of her? You bet. Do I pay her back in manual labor? Of course.

Beba did not start out as a vintner. She was a doctor and a mother. What a mother! She has twelve children. When Beba gave birth to child number eight, she knew she had to make a decision. She couldn't keep up her work as a doctor, make three meals a day, do the housework, and be a mother to all the children. Something had to give. She gave up housework. That's where I come in. When I visit the Freys, there is more than enough work to keep me occupied.

My biggest job at the Frey Ranch was helping with the wedding of daughter number two, Julia, who was getting married in the redwood grove on the property, as have most of her brothers and sisters. I arrived three weeks before the big day. The groom's relatives from Chicago would be staying in the "Big House," which had been the family home until the family expanded into other houses built on the same property. I painted, organized bedding, arranged furniture, hung Navajo rugs, fixed lamps, and in three weeks had the place looking like a southwestern bed and breakfast.

The wedding was worthy of *Bride Magazine*. Ten groomsmen and bridesmaids, two matrons of honor, and eight flower girls were in the wedding party. The bride arrived at the redwood grove seated on a white horse, flanked by her eight brothers in tuxedos. A bagpiper played in honor of the Scottish groom, a sixteen-voice chorus from San Francisco sang during the service, and a mariachi band decked out in white and gold outfits provided dance music at the reception. The wedding would have been fascinating to any bystander, but I got to be more than a bystander. All my hard work made me part of this scene.

Spending a few weeks in a place like the Frey Ranch or with family members not only gives me a break from my travels, but also allows me to live in someone else's routine. But after a few weeks looking at redwood groves, or tooling around in a Honda, or catching up with Larry King, I am ready to head back out on the open road.

six

By Land or Sea

*I asked the receptionist at the motel in Durham,
North Carolina where the nearest bus stop was.
She looked at me as if I were demented.
"You don't have a car?" she asked incredulously.
"No, I don't."
"We don't have bus information. No one uses the
bus. You'll have to speak to one of the chamber
maids. They ride the buses. But we don't advise
you to ride the bus."*

I n my eighteen years of travel, I have taken every kind of transportation from a dogsled to the Queen Elizabeth 2 luxury liner, and just about everything in between. Some of my best travel stories are about the process of getting to a destination.

The first seven years of my traveling life were dominated by boats. I had claustrophobia and could not get on an airplane, so when I wanted to go to Europe or Asia or Haiti, my only option was to go by ship, a very interesting way to travel.

Despite the hefty price tag, going to England on the luxurious ocean liner, the Queen Elizabeth 2, was a wondrous experience. The QE2 sailed between Southampton, England and New York City from May to November. This was traveling in the most incredible extravagance imaginable with a price tag to match ($1200). But there were still deals to be had. It is cheapest to travel during the first and last trips of the season and to stay in the rooms farthest down, with no portholes. There is so much to do on an ocean liner that it doesn't matter how far down your room is or how sparsely it is furnished. I was never in my room except for sleeping and changing my clothes.

I spent my time in the luxurious dining rooms where all my resolutions about not eating too much went straight overboard. There was a library outfitted with soft, leather furniture and an excellent selection of books, magazines, and newspapers. Tea was served twice a day in the Queen's Lounge. There was a room just for writing letters, a club where a band played nightly and chorus girls danced and sang, a movie theatre showing films twice a day, an indoor and outdoor pool filled with heated salt water, Turkish baths, saunas, a fitness center, beauty salons, barber shops, and a complete shopping mall. The QE2 is a floating city.

I was aboard her in July 1981 as the fairy tale wedding of Princess Diana and Prince Charles took place in St. Paul's Cathedral. It was called The Royal Wedding Cruise. We dined on Princess Diana Turkey and Prince Charles Steak. Each guest was given a silver medallion of the Princess and Prince in profile. The Captain gave a champagne party for all passengers. We raised our glasses in salute to the new couple and sang a teary "God Save the Queen."

The next day a helicopter dropped a video of the entire wedding on the deck of the QE2. We all rushed to the movie theatre to see this historic event. It was hard to believe that though we were out on the Atlantic we could still be part of Diana and Charles' wedding just twenty-four hours later.

I made this transatlantic voyage four times. I thank my claustrophobia for forcing me to take the QE2. Now I can cross the Atlantic in six hours instead of five days for less than half the money. And for less than half the fun.

I made another Atlantic crossing on the Stefan Batory, a small Polish passenger ship going from Montreal to Rotterdam. My first

44

reaction on seeing the Stefan Batory was, "Well, I'm not going on that tub. It'll never make it across the Atlantic Ocean." It's one-fourth the size of the QE2, and she was my standard for all ships. Fortunately, I quickly met a woman who was also sailing on the Stefan Batory. She seemed like a reasonable person, and I figured if she was willing to take the chance, I would, too.

There were 500 passengers aboard, mostly Poles, stocky, flat-faced women wearing babushkas, a sprinkling of Germans and Americans, and the rest English and Canadian. My cabin consisted of four berths with toilets and showers down the hall. It was easy to meet people because the ship was small. The food was heavy Eastern European fare: eel stew, borscht, boiled potatoes, thick pan-cakes, sauerkraut, fried cabbage, and bread.

As we set sail at four o'clock one afternoon, a few musicians played some Polish folk songs. Polish beer was eighty cents for a big bottle, sixty cents for Polish liqueur. Little bars and sitting rooms were spread throughout the ship. The entertainment was low-key. There was an hour of live classical music every morning and an hour of taped music in the afternoon. The captain inspected the ship daily, right down to placing a gloved finger in each ashtray, so the ship was immaculate. No, it was not the QE2, but it was a sur-prisingly nice way (and at $700, a far cheaper way) to make the Atlantic crossing.

I found one of my biggest ship bargains in Helsinki, Finland. I saw a sign advertising a four-day trip to St. Petersburg, Russia. I didn't even need a Russian visa because I wouldn't sleep on Russian soil. I slept on the boat in the St. Petersburg harbor.

I lined up for a ticket. "That will be $61.33," said the ticket agent.

"To St. Petersburg? For four days, meals included?"

"That is correct."

It was a very elegant ship. I had my own cabin with a porthole, complete bath, and all meals. Wine was served with lunch and din-ner. The waiters wore tuxedos. The tablecloth and napkins were made of linen. When I took a tour bus from the boat dock I was provided with a bag lunch. I had stumbled into a fantastic bargain.

It was a Baltic Line passenger ship named M/S Konstantin-Simonov. The ship carried two hundred eighty passengers out of a possible five hundred. Since I bought my ticket right at the harbor and there were still vacancies, I got the rock-bottom price.

I asked a couple on board what they had paid for this trip.

"Four-hundred dollars each," the man said pointing to himself and his wife. He had bought his tickets from a travel agent months ago back in America. I didn't ruin his trip by telling him what I had paid.

This is not uncommon, by the way. I often find my best bargains after I leave America. If I were on a two-week time schedule, covering twelve countries in Europe, I could forget about searching for bargains, but with my flexible approach to travel, I can seize any good opportunity that arises.

Back to Russia. Each day tour buses lined up on the dock to take us to the Hermitage, city hall, a tour of St. Petersburg, a ballet, a piano recital, and shopping on Nevsky Prospekt for the famous hand-painted lacquer boxes and the *matryoshka*, or nesting dolls. We also went to the Nikolai Palace to see the incredible Cossacks dance and sing. During intermission we were served red and black caviar with champagne. Another tour brought us to St. Nicholas Church where a wedding was taking place in one corner of the church, a funeral in another corner, a High Mass upstairs in an environment of pure gold.

This turned out to be the easiest and most pleasant way to get my foot inside Russia. I thought about repeating this excursion the next weekend just to live in luxury at $15 a day, but other adventures beckoned.

It was my eighteen-day trip to Yokohama, Japan, on a freighter that finally pushed me to conquer my claustrophobia. My goal was to get to Taegu, South Korea; and without being able to fly, the freighter was my only option. The freighter cost $1600, and then

I still had to take an overnight train to Kumamoto on the southernmost island of Japan, then a hovercraft to Pusan, Korea, and another train to Taegu. Final cost of the trip: $2000.

Freighters have erratic schedules, and I had no choice but to conform to their sailing dates. I had just gotten on board the freighter, a Chilean ship with an Indian crew, to begin the seventeen-day journey to Yokohama, when it was announced that there would be a delay of twenty-four hours while more freight was hoisted aboard. Now the trip was up to eighteen days.

But how to fill eighteen days? On this particular journey I was the only passenger. By law, the ship had to have a steward aboard to take care of the passengers' needs, whether there was one passenger or twelve, the maximum allowed. So I had the chief steward all to myself. He loosened the cap on the ketchup bottle for me. He poured the wine. He slid my chair in when I sat down to eat. Two waiters always stood at attention watching every bite go down so they could judge when to bring on the next course. I had a comfortable cabin to myself. For that matter, I had the entire passengers' lounge to myself along with hundreds of videos, old books, and magazines. Still, time passed very slowly. Watching two videos per day is about all I can bear. Some days I watched my first video at 7 a.m. The selection of books was uninteresting, but I read till I was blind trying to pass the time. I wrote letters. I walked the decks. I studied the ocean. So the next eighteen days passed very, very slowly.

Finally the port of Yokohama came into view, but I still had to confront the trains and the hovercraft before I got to Taegu.

When it was time to return to the US, I asked myself, "Do you really want to go through this whole silly, complicated, expensive procedure to get back home?" If I flew, I could be in San Francisco in ten hours instead of a month. The cost would be $700 instead of $2,000. What should I do? Could I finally cure myself of this irrational phobia?

I gave myself a stern lecture: "Dicky, it is time you put a stop to this infantile behavior. Why don't you be kind to yourself and board a plane like millions of other people do? Grow up!"

And I did.

I opted for mental health and bought a ticket on a plane out of Kimpo Airport in Seoul to San Francisco. Just to ensure victory, I took half a tranquilizer every hour starting four hours before flight time. I instructed my friend, Yoon, to keep pushing me towards the airplane door and not to allow me to change my mind. I bought a Business Class ticket so I wouldn't be packed in with the sardines. I knew I'd be given a Mimosa, champagne and orange juice, as soon as I appeared on the plane and that would be followed by another one. I gulped them both down.

Surprise! The flight was exceedingly comfortable. My seat was on the upper deck of the plane. To get there I walked up a spiral staircase which felt very luxurious.

What had been my problem all these years? This was a great way to travel. Ten hours later I was in San Francisco. I had conquered my claustrophobia.

Being able to fly opened up many new adventures for me. One of the best was "The Freedom Passport" from Continental Airlines for $999. This Passport entitled me to visit one American city each week for sixteen weeks. That figures out to $62.43 per trip. Florida to Oregon—$62.43. Los Angeles to North Carolina—$62.43. Always trying to get my money's worth, I even flew long flights to get more meals on the plane.

Armed with my hostel book in one hand and my Freedom Passport in the other, I set out to see sixteen new cities in sixteen weeks. In a week's time I could easily see all the main sights and pick up the ambience of any American city, with the exception of New York City; New York requires weeks.

So where did I go?

City #1: Our glorious capitol, Washington, D.C. The hostel there was within sight of the capitol dome and adjacent to a burned-out building, which seemed to be the story of this city. My week's lodg-

48

ing cost $126 with cooking privileges. This was definitely a bargain as I could walk to every major attraction in D.C., almost all of which are free.

From my congressman, I got free tickets to President Bill Clinton's Second Inauguration. I was seated in the same section as John F. Kennedy Jr. and his new bride, Carolyn, Johnny Cochran and Gil Garcetti of O. J. trial fame. As I left D.C. for Las Vegas, singer Michael Bolton boarded the plane.

City #2: Las Vegas, Nevada. This city can only happen in America. Sure, it has its sleazy aspects and it does feel decadent seeing people clutching their cups of coins as their eyes stay riveted on the one-armed bandit screen. But there is so much to see. Like Hotel New York, New York. It's in the shape of the N.Y. skyline with the Empire State Building, the Chrysler Building, the Brooklyn Bridge, for heaven's sake, a fireboat spraying water from the East River, and the Cyclone roller-coaster thrown in for good measure. And that's just one hotel.

It's not public knowledge but you can easily spend a week in Las Vegas without spending a nickel on a slot machine. My money went for cheap buffet breakfasts ($5.50) and dinners ($7.50), Nathan's hot-dogs, and an all-day tour to the Hoover Dam. My time went to enjoying the incredible interior decorations of these hotels and watching the tourists throw their money away.

Even though I had gone around the world and seen the Seven Wonders, this town still blew me away.

I didn't lose a nickel in Las Vegas.

City #3: South Beach, Florida. The hostel was the former Hotel Clay and cost $70 for the week. It was two blocks from the beach and boardwalk, ten blocks from the ritzy hotels (like the Fontainebleau), a ten minute walk from Versace's former villa, and right in the heart of the Art Deco District where all the hotels are painted in pastel shades.

49

In South Beach, I sometimes had to remind myself that I was still in America. Orthodox Jews have their own hotel there; the men in their black suits and hats, reading the Yiddish newspaper, provided quite a contrast to the rest of the beach goers. The women stood out, too. Among the bikini-clad, they wore their snoods, long-sleeved dresses, and stockings. And everyone else in South Beach seemed to speak Spanish. But over a bowl of black bean soup in a Cuban restaurant, I reminded myself that this is the kind of scene that makes up the American mosaic.

City #4: New Orleans and Mardi Gras. I didn't make a reservation at the official hostel in time so had to settle for an independent hostel with its sagging bed, overflowing trash baskets, and depressing environment. But I planned to spend no time there anyway.

The first night I saw six parades. As the floats in the parade went by, the people on the floats threw brightly colored strings of beads to the spectators. "There's no way I'm going to demean myself crawling around on the sidewalk trying to pick up beads like some beggar," I said to myself. That indignant feeling lasted about 45 seconds. I crawled, I grabbed, I fought for the necklaces and ended up with 360 strings. It was like finding the Hope Diamond.

The big cry was "Show me your tits." That gets you a string of beads. Fortunately, the lovely St. Louis Cathedral in the French Quarter was close by and the priests were happy to forgive your sins.

At one point, a truck with twenty convicts in orange jumpsuits pulled up, the name of the prison clearly printed on each jumpsuit. These men helped move barricades to control the crowd. Now and then a passerby would give the convicts the Black Power salute. A little unsettling but another picture of life in America.

City #5: Portland, Oregon. I caught the city bus to downtown Portland for 45 cents. The Visitors' Bureau gave me a city map and directions to the YWCA where I had a nice dormitory room for $13 a night in a perfect location, the heart of downtown. The city is bright, clean, and friendly. Here I visited some of America's natural wonders, taking a Gray Line Bus Tour to Mt. Hood and another to Mt. St. Helens.

City #6: Raleigh-Durham-Chapel Hill. Back across the country for my free breakfast and lunch aboard Continental Airlines to the Raleigh, Durham, and Chapel Hill area of North Carolina. There was no hostel in this area so I broke my rule and stayed in a motel. Despite the desk clerk at the motel warning me against using the buses, I found them efficient, air-conditioned, and driven by kind drivers who would answer any question courteously. Riding the buses gave me a chance to listen to and talk to many different people. As the only white person on the bus, I discovered another American language: Ebonics. I couldn't understand most conversations I eavesdropped on. If I asked a black person for information, she spoke so I could understand but then reverted to Ebonics when she turned back to her friend.

I tried to take a tour of the Liggett and Myers Cigarette factory, but they had their factory complex completely secured. I walked into the lobby which was completely empty and a disemboweled voice came over the loudspeaker asking what I wanted. Speaking up into the air I said I would like to take a tour of the factory. The voice said, "There are no tours available." An industry under siege.

City #7: Minneapolis and St. Paul, Minnesota. Here I tried a different kind of lodging. I called the College of St. Catherine's in St. Paul, a Catholic women's college. Yes, they had rooms for $15 a night. I had a private single room with a bathroom across the hall. The lovely, quiet campus was a ten minute walk from the mighty Mississippi.

The big attraction there is The Mall of America, the biggest shopping complex in the USA. It has a beach within the mall with waves rolling in, a complete amusement park called Camp Snoopy, food courts, entertainment, and every store known to an American. Shoppers from England fly in for a four-day weekend, shop till they drop, and still think they saved major money in spite of having flown over the Atlantic Ocean to get here.

City #8: Detroit, Michigan, the halfway point, and a week off to visit with my sister, Bempie. My head was spinning!

City #9: Salt Lake City, Utah. To get a feel for the Mormon religion (the fastest growing religion in America) a trip to Salt Lake City and Temple Square is a must. The Mormons couldn't be friendlier. They are a great addition to the medley that makes up America. But I did have to protect myself from these over-zealous folks. When I went down the escalator in a Mormon museum, I spotted two smiling faces at the bottom wanting to engage me in conversation. When I stepped out of the elevator on the Observation Deck in Temple Square, the next Mormon missionary in line jumped up from her seat to welcome me. These were all well-meaning, dedicated volunteers, but I am comfortable with my own religious views and often hid behind a statue or ducked into a restroom to escape their entreaties.

A visit to Salt Lake has to include the world famous Mormon Tabernacle Choir. I attended their rehearsal which takes place in the main Temple, and I sat in on Sunday morning services when they made their international radio broadcast.

City #10: New York City. I said I could not do NY in a week and I certainly can't sum up my visit to NY in a few sentences, but a few bargains deserve to be mentioned. New York City's hostel functions like a well-oiled machine. It's kept immaculately clean by the new immigrants who have come to make their home with us. I chose not to use the tiny self-catering kitchen because with innumerable ethnic restaurants—Arabian, Jewish, Italian, Spanish, Chinese, and mobile carts serving coffee and doughnuts or bananas and apples—

who wants to cook in a small, dark kitchen, anyway?

Where this hostel shines is in the activities it plans for its guests each week. They're all printed up and posted in the lobby. Most of the tours are free.

One walking tour took me to the Cathedral of St. John the Divine, on to Columbia University and through Harlem (which is now safe), and finally lunch at Sylvia's, the most famous restaurant in Harlem.

Another tour took me to see the Rikki Lake Show, another to the Bill Cosby Show, which was far more entertaining than Rikki. I could also have taken tours to 34th Street and the Empire State Building, to Wall Street and the Stock Exchange, to the Brooklyn Bridge for a stroll, to Chinatown, by ferry, past the Statue of Liberty and Ellis Island, to the Lower East Side where the Jewish immigrants came to settle.

An unusual and eye-opening experience was volunteering in a soup kitchen. The hostel told me exactly where to go. I took three different subways to reach Nativity Church near the Bowery to volunteer to serve a Saturday dinner.

The menu that Saturday—as it has been every Saturday for eleven years—is meatloaf topped with beef-stew, green beans, salad, mashed potatoes, and fruit.

As a volunteer, I attended a short orientation session so I would understand the principles under which this soup kitchen operated.

Principle No. 1. The people who ate there were only to be referred to as guests.

Principle No. 2. The volunteers were to eat the same food as the guests. We ate first so the guests could see that we did, indeed, eat the same food.

Principle No. 3. The guests were to be served immediately upon sitting down.

We served 450 people that day, mostly black men. The volunteers were all white with one exception. We worked for three hours.

One new, innocent volunteer making her first foray into the real world burst out crying when someone called her a "motherf . . ."

I got a front row seat to *Chicago* for $20 and a SRO ticket for *Lion King* by being in line at the box office at 9:30 a.m. the day of the performance. While waiting for the box office to open, I became acquainted with those in line around me, experiencing that famous New York friendliness. I met Felix Pire who was in a one-man show off-Broadway called *Man on the Verge of Having a His-panic Breakdown*. He said he'd set aside a free ticket for me since we were now friends. I went to his show and it was as good as *Chicago*.

I also heard Mayor Giuliani give a pep talk. He has radically changed the face of New York. I felt completely safe there. Ten years ago I wouldn't have gone down in a subway for fear I'd never come back out. Now there was no problem. That includes the Times Square neighborhood which used to be lined with porno shops, schizophrenics, and drug users. There are those who resent having Mickey Mouse on Times Square. They like the sleaze and raw edge better. I'm with Mickey.

City #11: San Juan, Puerto Rico. I found the Arcade Guest House one block from the beach for $50 per night. Ouch! But Puerto Rico has no budget accommodations as tourism is too important for bringing in the dollars.

I met two women from Argentina who wanted to rent a car but had never driven one with an automatic shift. They asked me to do the driving. I was happy to oblige and drove them all over the island to famous caves, through the rural countryside, and to temples where monkeys clamored on the roofs. We covered over half the island in that one day.

City #12: San Francisco, California. What I remember most vividly about San Francisco is the letter I wrote to Mayor Willy Brown about the panhandlers, the homeless pushing grocery carts stacked sky-high with plastic bags filled with who knows what, and the schizophrenics talking to themselves or shouting obscenities to some imaginary person.

"You got some change, lady?"

"Ma'am, can you spare a quarter?"

"God bless you and have a nice day."

I encountered eleven of these people on my ten-minute walk from the hostel on Mason Street to Borders Book Store. There they sat on a blanket on the sidewalk with a dog, dangling a cigarette, and holding a drinking cup from McDonald's. And they're asking *me*, fifty years older, for money? This was annoying to me and demeaning to them. I'd think they'd have more pride than to beg from a senior citizen who's living on Social Security. At the time of my visit we were in a great economic boom, and I had to wonder why this pathetic situation went on.

So I told Mayor Brown that at one time I considered San Francisco to be the most beautiful city in America. But I couldn't tell my fellow travelers that any longer.

He sent me a two-page letter explaining what a difficult problem this was. He and the city council were hard at work trying to solve this dilemma. I wish them all the luck in the world.

City #13: Phoenix, Arizona. I was not impressed. The hostel was dumpy and the city didn't seem to offer much aside from the beautiful campus of the University of Arizona. I did make a side-trip to the glorious Grand Canyon, so my time in Arizona was not a total waste.

City # 14: Memphis, Tennessee. I had never given a thought to visiting Graceland, the home of Elvis Presley. My parents had told us he was trash and we believed them. But my visit to Graceland changed all that. I felt I was entering an American Shrine.

When I first entered Elvis's home, I heard a lady behind me audibly gasp. I thought something had happened to her and quickly turned around. Her face was wreathed in a beatific smile as she gently put her foot down in Elvis's house and she sighed, "I can't believe I'm actually in *his* house!"

Contrary to my parents' assessment of Elvis, it was obvious that there were millions of people who loved him. They were in the souvenir shops snapping up pictures and mementos of him, laying flowers on his grave and his beloved mother Gladys's grave. Elvis's music played in the background.

At 72 years of age, I had to make a 180 degree turn and disagree with my parents. Elvis is not trash. He is an American icon.

City #15: San Antonio, Texas. I lucked out because the week I was in San Antonio was Fiesta Week. The city was draped in flowers, banners, and flags. Mariachi and ranchero bands played through the day and far into the night. Spirited parades took place. And it was all free.

City #16: Atlanta, Georgia. Last stop, my daughter's house, and time to mourn the end of a great continental tour. After these sixteen weeks, I had a much stronger feel for my country. I couldn't believe its incredible diversity. "From Sea to Shining Sea" became real for me.

Gordon Bethune, the CEO of Continental Airlines, was on the same plane with me on one of my many legs. I couldn't restrain myself from going up to him and saying, "Mr. Bethune, I'm traveling on a Freedom Passport and I *love* it."

Continental doesn't sell Freedom Passports any longer. Did I bring down their profit margin by taking sixteen trips at $62.43 per trip?

Another mode of travel that opened up for me when I conquered my claustrophobia was being an air courier for freight companies. All I needed was a valid passport, a deposit of $100, which I got back when I returned, and the ridiculously low price of my ticket. Contrary to what some might think, drugs are in no way connected with courier service. You are simply accompanying legitimate merchandise to its destination to ensure that it arrives when you do rather than being held up in customs.

The freight company didn't seem to care who I was—a pervert, an ex-criminal, or just a nerd. All the freight company was looking for was a warm body with a valid passport. What I did and where I stayed once I arrived at my destination was entirely up to me. I was hoping I would get to carry an attaché case handcuffed to my wrist, but no luck. The other passengers had no idea I was traveling as an air courier.

My first trip cost $100 round-trip and took me to Singapore for two weeks. The most spectacular orchid gardens and zoo are there. I can no longer visit any other zoo because they are so inferior to the one in Singapore.

Another courier flight took me to Hong Kong for a hundred dollar bill, and from there I took a short flight to Taiwan. The price of my next trip was higher, $450, but that got me to the Southern Hemisphere and the continent of Australia. Another $100 flight took me to Milan, Italy. And yet another took me to Ireland.

My most exciting flying experience—and the one that proved to me once and for all that I had conquered my claustrophobia—was flying over the Arctic Circle in a Piper Cub. I was staying at Grandma Shirley's Hostel in Fairbanks, Alaska, and yes, I was older than Grandma Shirley. I met Sarah, a woman from New Zealand, who told me that her life's ambition was to get to the Arctic Circle. Her plan was to tag along on a two-hour plane trip delivering mail and passengers to two small native villages north of the Arctic Circle. The cost was $165. Would I please go with her?

"Oh, sure," I confidently responded since the trip was still a week off. We made our reservations.

When the day actually dawned, my heart started pounding. I had conquered my claustrophobia, but that was in business class. How would I do in a plane fit for four passengers, the pilot, and a supply of groceries? When we boarded the plane, there were two other passengers, native women who came to Fairbanks once a month to do their grocery shopping. Our pilot, Gary, climbed into the plane through the window. We were seated right behind him.

I always carry a small supply of tranquilizers in my fanny-pack just in case I get trapped in an elevator or have some other emergency.

This was an emergency.

How did I get talked into this trip in a tin can by a woman I had just met at Grandma Shirley's Hostel?

I slipped half a tranquilizer into my mouth as we took off for the frozen North.

I engaged the two native women in conversation to get my mind off what was happening. The one woman said she had lived in the first village we would stop at for twenty years, but it had gotten too crowded for her. It had grown to a population of two hundred. Now she was living in the smaller village where there were only seventy people, and it was much more peaceful.

As I looked down at the deathly silent, cold land far below, I took another piece of tranquilizer. It got stuck in my throat. One of the native ladies was drinking a Sprite. Being desperate I asked her for a swallow. She graciously handed me her bottle.

Later Sarah asked me how I could have been so nervy to ask a stranger for a drink from her bottle.

When we landed at the first village above the Arctic Circle, we stayed for twenty minutes to unload cargo and pick up new cargo. One of the two women left us, and we picked up a Japanese tourist who had spent several nights there watching the Aurora Borealis or Northern Lights. We landed in the second village in a snow storm. Our next passenger arrived by snowmobile, driving right to the door of the plane.

You can get used to anything, the old saying goes, and by the time we were headed back to Fairbanks, flying over this desolate, lonely landscape was pure joy. I had pushed myself once again, taken a risk, and met a new ordeal head-on. This is the kind of experience that gives you renewed confidence and faith in yourself, I thought. I wanted to keep going higher and higher.

And then, when landing at the airport in Fairbanks, the right tire of our plane blew. We careened across the airstrip. Emergency vehicles arrived in two minutes to rush us back to the terminal.

But even this couldn't dull my joy. I was given a Certificate of Arctic Exploration which proclaimed: "This is to certify that on this, the 5th day of November in the year 1996, DICKY JENSEN traveled across the ARCTIC CIRCLE with Warbelow's Air Ventures," signed by Art Warbelow, President, Warbelow's Air Ventures, Inc.

A great gift to leave for my children since they won't be getting any money.

If flying over the Arctic Circle was the zenith of my travel experiences, riding the Greyhound bus was the nadir. I had fond memories of the Greyhound; I had crisscrossed the country with my children on the Greyhound when it was still an efficient, acceptable way to travel. It breaks my heart to tell the truth about traveling on the Greyhound bus these days. It is the most uncomfortable, frustrating, and unpredictable way to travel.

I'm not talking about the prices because they are unbeatable. I'm not talking about the drivers because almost every one is courteous, professional, and well dressed.

I'm talking about how we customers are treated. We are treated as if we belong to the lowest level of society, like cattle sent off to the slaughter.

My trip from Atlanta to Detroit is a case in point. I didn't buy my airline ticket in time and a last minute ticket cost $400. The Greyhound Bus ticket cost $56. The decision was easy.

When I bought my ticket at the Greyhound terminal, the agent said I would be leaving in an hour from Gate 4. I obediently stood in line for the hour at Gate 4.

When I got to the facilitator (the guy who takes your ticket), he asked, "Where are you going, ma'am?"

"To Detroit."

"Gate 9."

"I was told Gate 4. See, it's written on my ticket."

"Gate 9."

I obediently went over to Gate 9 where I had to wait another hour and a half. I didn't try to find out why this was so. There was no explanation. I had entered the Underbelly of America.

I never believe a driver when he says, "We'll have a half-hour rest stop here. Be back on the bus in 30 minutes." What he actually means is 60 minutes. Or 70 minutes. Or an hour and a half. There is no way to know. The passenger is completely at the mercy of the Greyhound system, so I had to grit my teeth and do what I was told. When the bus got to Cleveland, the bus driver instructed the passengers to re-board in 30 minutes. We did. We sat there another 45 minutes wondering when the bus driver would show up. When he did, he was not happy.

"Who let you people on the bus? It's against the law to board the bus without having your tickets checked!"

We sat there like dumb cattle.

"I'm going to the office about this," he went on. "And I'm not sure I want to drive this bus. It's filthy. I don't drive filthy buses."

The cattle said nothing.

Soon he was back with the next instructions.

"Now listen up. I want all you people off this bus. I want you to stand behind that last glass door until I tell you to get back on the bus. This bus is going to be cleaned. I don't drive filthy buses."

The cattle got off the bus and took their places behind the designated glass door and waited.

After we were allowed back on the bus the driver gave us the usual instructions.

"No drinking alcoholic beverages, no use of any drugs, no loud music. If you have anything to say, don't shout at me from the back of the bus. Walk up to me and tell me politely what you want." Then he added, "The toilet in the back of the bus is for emergency use only. If you have to make number two, you can hold it till we come to our next rest stop. That will be in three hours. If you just have to urinate, it's okay to use the toilet."

That's life in the Underbelly of Transportation, also known as the Greyhound Bus Line.

Was it worth it to save $344? Probably. I still check Greyhound every time I plan to make a trip in the US, but that is mostly because of nostalgia. Now that flying has become so common and so much cheaper, and now that I have conquered my claustrophobia, the airplane is always a better option.

From the big dogs on a dogsled to the Big Dog of Greyhound, I have experienced just about every mode of transportation available. Some of them have been the height of luxury while others have been the pits, but they all add up to more adventure, and that is my goal.

seven

One Head is Better than Two

I told one woman about my traveling lifestyle.
She sighed and said, "Oh, I wish I could do what
you do!"
"Why can't you?"
"I have three grandchildren nearby. And I get to
see them almost every day."
"Well, kiss your grandchildren goodbye. Tell them
you'll be sending them postcards and you'll be
back in about six months."
"Oh, I could never do that," she said.
"Then you can't do what I do."

One of my cardinal rules of travel is *Travel Alone*. If I travel with someone else, strangers will not talk to me. It's that simple. If I travel alone, everyone talks to me and I talk to everyone. My travels are infinitely enriched. I can always talk to my best friend, my sisters, or my grandchildren when I spend a few weeks at their houses. When I travel I want to get to know the natives.

"But aren't you lonely?" I am always asked.

I am never lonely. I talk with people all day. I ask them questions. I ask for directions. I make up questions to get a conversation started. At night, I'm at a hostel and have anywhere from four to ten roommates with whom to discuss the happenings of the day. When I cook dinner in the self-catered kitchen, I simply say to another hosteler standing over the stove, "Boy, that looks good. What is it?" Or "That smells great!" And conversations ensue. Most people in non-English speaking countries are anxious to improve their English and will latch onto you immediately when they realize they can practice on you.

I've met great people, many of whom became my best friends, because I was *alone*. I can't emphasize this point enough.

That's how I met Karen Tham in Singapore. Stopping to rest after walking all over the city, I was soon joined by this tired Singaporean lady with groceries. We began to chat about the weather. This led to "Where are you from?" and then to "Why don't you come to my apartment for some cold water?" I got to see a typical Singaporean home. I heard all about her family and what her husband did for work. She served me a special Singaporean dessert of herbal jelly with seed pods and honey on top. It actually looked quite disgusting; the gray, lumpy pods looked like slugs. It was nothing I would have ordered in a restaurant, but I managed to down most of it. She refilled my water bottle, gave me two bananas, and walked me to the bus stop.

Two days later, Karen picked me up in her new air-conditioned car, and off we went to see Little India, a downtown neighborhood. While there, we noticed a crowd gathered outside the Tamil Hall and stopped to see what was going on. "It's a wedding," we were told. "Please, come in." After only a moment's hesitation, we did just that.

The wedding was gorgeous. To the constant beating of drums and blowing of horns, the odor of incense, and the video camera thrust right into the face of the traditionally dressed priest and bridal couple, we watched the blessings being laid on the heads of the bride and groom. The bride was absolutely gorgeous in her gold jewelry which started at the top of her head and went right down to her bare feet. Since so many people were coming in and going out, we felt comfortable leaving after an hour so we could explore more of Little India. When we returned to our car after two hours, the wedding was just coming to a close.

Karen Tham is still my good friend, and anytime I go to Singapore I can call her and arrange another interesting day. I met Karen simply because I was alone.

That's also how I met Sam in Hong Kong, Ann Ings from the UK, Sookjin from South Korea, Pippi from Israel, Milan from the Czech Republic, Lu Song from China and all the other people in my fat, black address book.

Take my friend Sigi. While living in Marburg, Germany, I noticed that there was another person renting a room across the hall from my apartment. I didn't know who it was but decided to find out. I went to the door, knocked, and there stood a lovely, 21-year-old woman.

I said, "Hi. I'm living across the hall and I just wanted to say hello."

"Oh, are you American?" she asked with excitement. "Come in."

At that moment began a wonderful friendship. Sigi, short for Sigrunne, and I are still friends seventeen years later. She told me she was dating an American soldier and he stayed with her on weekends. My immediate reaction was, "Oh, an American soldier taking advantage of a young German woman. He just wants a nice place to come for the weekend and a nice warm body to snuggle up to. Nothing is ever going to come of this."

Of course, I was wrong.

Her boyfriend's name was Diego. He was a Puerto Rican who was adopted into a Jewish family, the Wolborskys.

In Germany they call the Americans *Amis*, a derogatory term. Sigi's parents told her that if she married that *Ami* they would never speak to her again.

She said, "Well, I love him and I'm going to marry him." And she did. The family didn't speak to her for years, but finally they came around. They realized she was happy. She gave them two grandchildren, David and Emily.

I visited Sigi as she followed Diego to each of his new stations: in El Paso, Texas; in Colorado Springs; and again to Germany.

The point of this story is simple. Why was I able to meet this interesting woman and have my life enriched by knowing her? The reason I met Sigi is that I was alone. If I had a traveling companion would I have gone across the hall? No. But I needed someone to talk to and found Sigi.

I also make many friends while standing at a bus stop. It didn't take me long to figure out that Germans, or most nationalities, for that matter, will never speak to a stranger first. I had to start the conversation. At the bus stop, I would pick out an unsuspecting victim and say something innocuous like, *Regnet es heute?* (Will it rain today?) or *"Um wieviel Uhr kommt der Bus?"* (What time will the bus come?). "Do you speak English?" is another good question to get a conversation going.

With these simple sentences, the ice is broken. The person's face lights up, and I am on my way to making a new acquaintance. I picked out Johan Schneider, a 90-year-old man, at a bus stop in Germany. He was very happy to talk with me as he had met Americans during World War II. He invited me to his house to show me his scrapbooks and memorabilia of the war years. And, yes, I went. He was 90, after all. He lived in a cozy apartment downstairs from his daughter and her husband, a doctor. As we were looking through his scrapbooks, the daughter came downstairs to see who was talking with her father. She asked me suspiciously, "What are you doing here?" I told her that I was an American living in Marburg. I had met her father at a bus stop and he invited me to visit him. We were having a nice chat.

She figured I had some ulterior motive. She invited me to come upstairs to join her and her husband for dinner so she could check me out.

"Oh, no thank you. I just came over to talk with your father."

"Well, when you're ready to go home, I'll have my husband drive you." Somehow she was going to find out what I was all about.

So the doctor drove me back to my apartment, and I made it a point to invite him in to see how I lived. I also made it a point to mention my landlord's name since he was a judge; he lived upstairs and I knew that would give me credence. I obviously passed the test because I was invited back for coffee, a rather stiff affair with linen tablecloth and napkins. Later I was invited to a beautiful Sunday dinner.

So the American lady wasn't trying to seduce the old father, after all. When I left Germany, they presented me with a German Bible as a gift for having brought some pleasure into the old man's life.

For every story I have of the people I've met because of traveling alone, I can tell a story about best friends setting off on a trip together only to return as mortal enemies.

"Okay, let's go see the sights," says Traveler A after breakfast. "But I have to take a shower," says Traveler B. And the seething begins.

Each person has his own rhythm, and the best place to see how rhythms differ is on a trip. I advise couples who are planning to marry to first go on a three-week trip. If the couple survives the trip, the chances are the marriage will also survive.

Rose and Cheri started out from Taiwan as best buddies. They had planned a great trip to China to visit Cheri's parents. When next I met Cheri, she and Rose were not speaking to each other. They hadn't even seen each other in a year.

"All Rose wanted to do was go sightseeing, but I wanted to visit with my parents," complained Cheri.

An Italian traveler, Mary Grace, told me how she and her girl-friend had started out their trip arm in arm as they got on the train. At the end of the trip, the girls sat on opposite sides of the train, studiously ignoring each other.

The one time I broke this rule was an unqualified disaster.

I was invited by my brother to join him and three friends on a tour of the Pyramids of Egypt, a sail up the Nile to the famous archeological digs, a week in Israel, and finally a week in Istanbul, Turkey. I should have known not to get mixed up with three fellow travelers, but I didn't think I would feel comfortable in Cairo by myself. And wasn't it thoughtful that I was invited to go along on this trip? So I allowed feelings to take over instead of straight, clear thinking. I joined a *Tour*. Big mistake.

We started as a friendly group at JFK International Airport while waiting to board our plane for Cairo. We ended up at the same airport three weeks later with my dashing out the nearest exit without saying goodbye to my brother or thanking him for inviting me on the trip. Our relationship was not the same for years.

It started out fine. Egypt is quite a place to visit. The Pyramids of Giza have to be the most exciting and unbelievable sight in the world. They are so monumental and so awe-inspiring that I caught my breath at first seeing them. And then I thought about them being built 5,000 years ago before any kind of sophisticated machinery was invented. The plateau on which the pyramids rest are filled with palm trees, camels, horses, donkeys pulling wooden wagons filled with red carrots, and Arab vendors dressed in traditional clothing. I felt like I was back in biblical times.

We walked across the bridge from Giza to Cairo, crossing the Nile, and then explored downtown. It was overwhelming and I congratulated myself for having come here with companions. We visited Memphis, the original capital from 5,000 years ago, and saw the huge statue of Ramses which was just recently discovered under the sand.

After our four-day trip up the Nile, our trip back into ancient history was over. We flew Royal Jordanian Airlines to Amman, Jordan and on to Israel. And then the trouble began.

I *never* check any luggage because it's too time-consuming to retrieve and there's always the remote possibility that it will be lost. But since the whole group was checking luggage, I didn't want to appear different (big mistake). I checked mine, too. Would I have done this had I been alone? No. The only baggage that didn't make it through to the Ben-Gurion Airport in Tel-Aviv was mine. I made out a lost-luggage form, completely confident that in a day or two a taxi would drive up to the French convent where we were staying and drop off my baggage.

By the fourth day, when I couldn't get any straight answers from anyone at the airport as to the whereabouts of my baggage, the trip went downhill fast. At one point I was told to meet a taxi at the Jaffa Gate, but when it got there, the bags were for Nielsen, not Jensen. Then I spent eight hours at the airport working with Henry, an airport baggage handler, trying to locate the elusive baggage. Yes, we've found your baggage at the airport in Amman. A sign of hope. Henry sent telexes which were not answered. He told me to wait for the 5:30 plane from Amman; perhaps my bag would arrive. Hope dashed again.

But the really discouraging part was that there was no support forthcoming from my group. My traveling buddies were saying things like, "Looking for your luggage will keep you off the streets," or "It'll give you something to do," or "It's only an hour to the airport, what's the problem?" when I made yet another trip to Ben-Gurion airport.

I spent hours at the Royal Jordanian Airline Office in East Jerusalem trying to get compensation. Finally they did give me a $50 bill which didn't begin to cover the hours spent at the airport and on the phone. While the group was seeing the sights, I was left to figure out my own problem.

I felt physically assaulted. If I had experienced this while traveling alone it would have been no problem. I would have figured out the solution by myself. But since I was a member of a group, I looked to them for help and support. I felt owed something by the group, and when the group didn't come through for me, I felt terribly let down. That is why I'll never break my *travel alone* rule again.

Finally on the next to last night of our week in Israel, I received a call that my baggage would be arriving at the Notre Dame Hotel outside the Damascus Gate. I set out in the rain, walked through the Beggars' Market, up the hill to Notre Dame. In a half hour a taxi pulled up and there was my baggage. It was an anticlimax to six days of frustration.

This is not to say that I never join up with a fellow traveler to take in some sights. Traveling in hostels, such short-term partnerships are common. Sometimes these temporary alliances can go wrong, but then I have no commitment or expectations of the people I am traveling with. It is easy to go my separate way. In a Phoenix hostel, I met two women from England who planned to rent a car and drive to Flagstaff and the Grand Canyon. Would I like to join? Most certainly.

On the second day we drove to have breakfast, a seemingly simple procedure.

"How about McDonald's or Burger King?" I asked.

"Those places are nothing but rubbish!" one woman countered.

"How about Denny's?"

"That's rubbish, too."

"Oh," I thought to myself. "I would never describe your beloved Marks and Spencer with that term!" I felt personally insulted for my favorite restaurants, the State of Arizona, and all of America, including Alaska and Hawaii.

So we drove down the main street as the fussy Brit dashed in and out of about three restaurants proclaiming they didn't have the right food.

"What exactly are you looking for?" I asked hoping to bring this big treasure hunt to a close.

"I won't know until I see it on the menu," came the unfathomable reply.

It was time to make my exit. "I'll tell you what, girls. I'll finish driving you to the Grand Canyon but then I'm jumping ship. I'm not going to spend an hour three times a day trying to figure out what you want to eat."

And that's exactly what I did. After enjoying the grandeur of the Grand Canyon I hopped a bus back to Phoenix, glad to be on my own again.

eight

Why I Don't Want Another Relationship

Because I am divorced and still single, I am asked constantly, "Don't you want another relationship?" The answer is a firm, unequivocal "No!" What for? I don't want to repeat my high school years, do I? I don't want to raise children again. So why would I want to repeat the marriage scene? I had a very satisfying marriage for twenty-nine-years, except for the final two weeks. But that chapter of my life is over.

There are other lifestyles besides the married one, especially today. Single women are not looked down on as being out of sync with society. Actually, it's the reverse. Now single women are looked up to and even envied. I know some married women who would love to trade places with their single friends. I was given a priceless opportunity when my husband announced that my Number One spot with him had been given to another woman. I didn't realize this at first, of course. Instead I wanted to die. I asked God to give me a little case of cancer that would be quick and painless.

My grief at the end of my marriage was, in part, a problem of identity. If I was no longer Mrs. Jensen, wife of Willy, then who was I? I felt like a nonentity floating around in the atmosphere high above the Earth. That was the most frightening part of the divorce.

But there are other identities, I discovered. I could be Dicky the English teacher in Taegu, Korea, Dicky the Peace Corps Volunteer, or simply Dicky the Traveler.

And besides, what would a man do for me?

I don't need money. I can earn my own money or rely on the money and health insurance my generous Uncle Sam provides for me. Besides, money isn't where fulfillment lies. And, realistically, how much money does a person need to keep body and soul together? Not very much. So getting access to some man's bank account is of no interest.

I don't need companionship. At one time it was nice to have someone say, "Hi, honey! How was your day?" But that time is over. Now I want to be asked, "What country are you visiting next?" Or "How was it in Hong Kong?" Living in hostels gives me all the companions I'll ever need. I meet a new group every day. They're from all over the world and have unique stories to tell and good advice to share. It is much more enriching to have limitless companions than one steady one.

I don't need someone for my old age. I don't have time to worry about what's going to become of me when I get old. I'm positive it will all work out. One thing is sure: I won't have to nurse a partner through a long, terminal illness.

I don't need a roof over my head. How lackluster to have the same roof over your head day after day. How exciting to have a different roof over your head every few days or weeks! And it's a roof you never have to worry about replacing!

I don't need sex. I think of all the celibate people in our world who live rich, fulfilling lives. And sex is strictly overrated. You'd think from looking at magazine covers and watching TV that it is the only game in town. It isn't.

No, I don't need any of these things. What I need is freedom. I graduated from high school; I launched my three children into the world; I signed my divorce papers. I don't need to return to any of these roles when there are so many more roles for me to explore.

nine

Taking Advantage of Friends and Relatives: China

In the spring of 1995, my nephew, John Kurth, then 28, got a job teaching English at the Hunan Medical School in Changsha, China, the capital of the Hunan Province. As soon as I heard this precious bit of news, I knew where my next adventure would take me. John was about to get a visit from his Aunt Dicky. As it turned out, I was his only relative to visit him. This shows how unimaginative people are about taking advantage of golden opportunities. And John speaks Chinese. Not even his mother or father hopped a plane for Changsha.

Yale University has a brick house on the Hunan Medical campus which houses the crop of students who volunteer to teach English for a year. There was an extra bed next to the washer and dryer, which was open for John's *gu-gu*, or aunt. The house had its own cook, Shao Fung, a young Chinese girl whose waist looked about ten inches around. She made a typical Hunan lunch each day, heavily seasoned with red pepper, which is what distinguishes the food in this province.

For the next three weeks I explored Changsha, a city of 2 million, and its environs. It was the perfect way to feel somewhat at ease with this new culture. I had my American base with people who spoke my language from which I could make forays into Chinese life. I had my interpreter, John, to help me with the harder aspects of travel in China.

The highlight of this visit was an invitation from the

Communist government to visit the Second International Bamboo Cultural Festival in Yiyang, a town two hours from Changsha. The government invited twenty foreigners and, as John's *gu-gu*, I was one of the lucky twenty.

We had no idea what a dazzling cultural experience awaited us in Yiyang. From the moment we arrived at our hotel to the sad farewell three days later, we were dined, entertained, escorted, and treated like royalty. Each of us was assigned our own room in the hotel although there were three beds in each room. When we first arrived we were driven in air-conditioned vans via police escort to the gymnasium to witness a two-hour spectacular of dancing and singing in honor of the bamboo tree.

A banquet followed; the first of many. Now, I had heard about Chinese banquets before but had no idea what they were like until I experienced one. No less than fourteen different dishes would be served at one meal, plate piled on top of plate as the table couldn't hold them all. I dined on sweet and sour pork with bean curd, lotus roots, pork and bamboo, spicy chicken, fried eel, Chinese spinach with garlic, cauliflower with mushrooms, a whole chicken which had to be dissected with chopsticks, and an entire fish. My cup and glass were continually refilled with a smoky jasmine tea and the local Yiyang beer. Fortunately I was always allowed an hour's rest after one of these orgies.

Communism was very evident at our visit to the Bamboo Forest. Fifty children, all with big smiles, were lined up on either side of our path holding flowered hoops and chanting, "Welcome to China!" How long had they been required to stand in the heat awaiting our arrival? These fifty children were followed by a band of thirty students in ornate white uniforms playing welcome music. Then another twenty teenaged girls, holding bamboo umbrellas, smiled a welcome for us. As soon as we were seated under umbrellas and given bottles of mineral water, the next extravaganza of dancing and singing commenced, after which we were given a boat ride on the nearby lake so we could get a closer look at the bamboo forests and

76

majestic mountain ranges.

In the meantime, the farmers from the surrounding villages became aware of what was going on and gathered to stare at us long-nosed foreigners. It was fascinating to watch the expressions on their faces as they scrutinized the hair on our arms, the length of our noses, and the color of our hair. We even walked differently, taking longer, more confident strides as if we owned the world. They stared unabashedly trying to figure out where these strange creatures had come from. Finally, one woman came up to me staring intently and asked, "Where you buy teeth?"

"No buy teeth. *My* teeth," I replied as I tapped them.
"Oh," she sighed. "Very beautiful."

Meanwhile the children who had greeted us had to wait around until we left several hours later so they could sing-song their chants again. I had to wonder if American children would be constitutionally able to spend a day like this. I had to conclude, "No way."

Then we were driven past rice paddies where the farmers were doing their backbreaking work as they planted each rice seedling by hand—enough to feed 1.2 billion people. The big, black water buffalo plowed up the mud. By way of a tortuous dirt road, we arrived on the top of a mountain where a huge teahouse awaited us. The tea served was only for VIPs as it had to be specially ground. It was served cold, was the color of dish water, and had peanuts floating on top. It was served with nine different snacks like seaweed, mango peel, and dried mushrooms.

Was that enough entertainment for one day? No! After yet another banquet we were taken back to the gymnasium for another three hour extravaganza in honor of the bamboo tree. This experience was a little scary for me as a fire-conscious Westerner. At least 10,000 people were jammed into this building. Every aisle and staircase was filled with sitting bodies. Not one open space could be seen. There were only three exit doors at either end and all the windows were covered with steel bars. I debated whether I should get hysterical on the spot or tough it out. I tried not to imagine the terrible scenarios that could take place. I stayed rooted in my seat, enjoyed the endless singing and dancing, the unbelievable costumes and props, and heaved a sigh of relief when I walked out into the night still intact.

Again I had to admire the patient Chinese children. There were many in the audience sitting on their parents' laps or on the concrete steps. They never moved. No one went to the bathroom. No one asked for water. No one asked for something to eat. Not one child made a sound for three hours.

We visited a museum of calligraphy, a museum specializing in sculptured roots, and a museum devoted to bamboo, of course. At the bamboo market we bought bamboo ladles, bamboo hand-carved spoons, bamboo pillows, bamboo umbrellas, bamboo slippers, bamboo bowls, bamboo cups, and bamboo vases. Yiyang is a bamboo world.

As our parting gift we were each given an inscribed tote-bag, baseball cap, tie clasp, bamboo picture frame, and a watch. The same one hundred children who had greeted our arrival sang their chanting songs at our departure. I felt like a foreign dignitary.

Another high point of my visit with John was visiting the Karst Mountains along the River Li. These are the strange but beautifully shaped mountains found in almost all Chinese landscape paintings. John and I decided to see these mountains in person. We took a "hard-sleeper" from Changsha for the eleven hour trip to Guillin. A "hard-sleeper" consists of six beds per compartment with no door. You get a reserved bed so there's no scrambling; we Westerners are no match for the Chinese when it comes to scrambling.

Since John had his father's credit card, I broke my hostel rule and we stayed on the eighth floor at the beautiful Holiday Inn in Guillin. We had a corner room with spectacular views of the mountains, the full moon, and the city. The hotel gave excellent service and was immaculate. We even found mints on our pillows.

Since Guillin is now a major tourist spot in China, the prices have soared. To take the hour and half cruise down the River Li cost $60, and the boat company wouldn't accept John's credit card. We tried different ships, looking for a better price. When one didn't turn up, we decided to take a minivan that drove parallel to the River Li. That cost $1.50 and we saw the same spectacular mountains. Coming back that evening in the same minivan, the light was perfect. The mountains were dramatically silhouetted against the evening sky. They looked ancient. They were China epitomized. It was an unparalleled trip; a real look at a Chinese landscape.

After three weeks in Changsha, John put me on the train to Beijing. As my train pulled out of the station, I reflected on the wisdom of taking advantage of my relatives. As his only visitor from home, I had made John happy, and I had had a spectacular introduction to China.

ten

Dicky in the Holy Land

t was an ordinary afternoon and I was poking around the Ackerman Student Union Building on the UCLA campus. I always pick up the student newspapers and read notices and posters around a college campus looking for new opportunities. That day, I was not disappointed. Glancing over a display case of brochures, my eye caught one that said: "If you've been waiting for a formal invitation to visit Israel, YOU'VE GOT IT! Volunteers for Israel."

I had never thought about Israel before, but as I perused the brochure, I saw a new trip opening up before me.

The brochure explained that the "primary purpose of this program is to provide aid to Israel through volunteer work and to build lasting relationships between Israelis and the Diaspora." A new word for me. We would participate in "various duties currently performed by overburdened Israelis, thus lightening their load by our efforts." They also offered "organized tours, educational lectures, evening programs, and much more." The key sentence in the whole brochure was: "Our program is available to the young and young-at-heart." That's me.

I wasted no time in calling the Volunteers for Israel office in New York City to request a packet of information.

Three days later I was poring over the packet. I learned that I would have to pay my own airfare (about $1000), I would live (for free) in army barracks with female soldiers, and I'd eat my three kosher meals each day in the soldiers' mess hall. I was also expected to work eight hours a day, five days a week, getting Friday and Shabbat (another new word for me) off. The kind of work I would be doing would depend on the "current need," including any of the following: manual labor, repair, maintenance, patient care, kitchen duties, gardening, and geriatric care. My assignment could be at a hospital, army or navy base, and it would last for three weeks.

I was warned that the "accommodations may not be up to [my] expectations," but the organization asked me to "accept them with understanding and a sense of humor, keeping in mind that the main objective of the program is to help Israel." Even the note attached to my medical certificate did not put me off:

Dear Doctor,

The following applicant has indicated a desire to serve with Volunteers for Israel. As our program is a rigorous 23 days which may involve Spartan living accommodations (e.g. army cots, no air conditioning), working in the hot sun, and repetitive lifting, bending, and long hours on one's feet, it is important that only those individuals who are in good physical condition with a stable positive mental outlook be approved. You will be doing your patient a disservice by approving them even if they are borderline as they may not be able to complete their assignment.

I was a 67-year-old gentile ready to head to the Holy Land for adventure. I wanted to get a handle on what exactly was going on in this world hot-spot. I hoped to have the unique experience of meeting and working closely with Israelis while getting an insider's view of the culture, lifestyle, and pulse of Israel.

I had to be interviewed by a rabbi to make sure I wasn't some kind of a religious freak who was going to cause trouble in Jerusalem. I found Rabbi Larry Halpern in the yellow pages. He interviewed me for an hour and then wrote me a recommendation affirming my sanity. I had to have a physical and I had to purchase health insurance. No problem.

I sent my completed application to New York City, and, a few days later, I received a call telling me which flight to take out of JFK aboard Tower Airlines. I was in. In no time, I was in New York City meeting my group of volunteers and winging my way toward Tel Aviv.

There were 22 volunteers in my group, two Christians: Tex from San Antonio and me. Some were young: two volunteers who had just graduated from Yale, one from Harvard, and one who was about to head off to Washington University in St. Louis. One 24 year-old woman was a born-again Jew. She used to smoke marijuana and now she wears stockings on Shabbat. And there were some gray-heads, too: a 60-year-old man who was on his fifth volunteer session and a man from New Jersey who owned a drapery factory employing 30 people. There was also a man in his forties who was definitely psychotic and wanted to rebuild Solomon's Temple on the Temple Mount. How did he get past the rabbi? (He actually ended up leaving early because "God spoke to him.") Israel hopes that a few of these volunteers will decide to make *aliyah* (another new word meaning to settle down in Israel) and 6% of volunteers do exactly that.

We were met at Ben Gurion Airport in Tel Aviv by a female Israeli soldier with her army bus. It was then that we were told our assignment. We would be members of the IDF, the Israeli Defense Force, and were to be stationed at the Neta Fim Army Base, one of the three bases making up the Northern Command. Neta Fim is in Tiberius, just twenty minutes from the Sea of Galilee. Suddenly I was in the land of my Sunday school stories. I remembered the picture of Jesus in a boat on the Sea of Galilee as he calmed the storm. Or when he had his disciple, Peter, cast out his net and come up with a net full of fish. And I was going to live twenty minutes away!

We were assigned to beds in the women's barracks, and the men got their assignments in the men's barracks. At the Quartermaster Building we were issued our uniforms. They were exactly like the ones the real soldiers wore—olive pants and shirt, black boots, gray wool socks, and a cap. The only difference was that we wore a blue ribbon on our left shoulder to indicate that we were volunteers and that we carried no weapons. I wished that ribbon was a little bigger!

One of our first nights there we had a terrorist drill. Six bedraggled soldiers with Uzi's slung over their shoulders rounded us up and escorted us to a specific room where we were to go if terrorists ever got on base.

We were given a tour of the eight huge warehouses on base which housed every conceivable part for tanks, trucks, cannons, and artillery. Then we received our work assignments. Most were assigned to the warehouses testing radio equipment, taking inventory, cleaning rust from camshafts and cannons. I lucked out because I was assigned to kitchen duty where I cut melons, tomatoes, and peppers, set 12 tables for three meals each day, brought out the soup course followed by the main course, cleared the tables, and washed dishes. I got innumerable coffee and melon breaks and my boss kept saying, "Go slowly. Take a rest." The other volunteers were jealous because they were inhaling dust and working around pigeon shit. One day four women took to their beds due to exhaustion and culture shock.

I quickly learned what eating kosher meant. We worked in two entirely separate kitchens. One was for dairy products and one was for meat products. I had saved a few leftover pieces of chicken one day, but when I later looked for them in the refrigerator, they were gone. Hey, what happened to my chicken? I had put it in the wrong refrigerator so the chicken was contaminated and had to be thrown out. The refrigerator had to be scrubbed clean. Another day a bee

 84

flew into my teacup and I had to boil the cup since the bee was considered meat.

One of my goals on this trip was to be in touch with real Israelis. That goal was easily met by the people I worked with. My wonderful boss, Nisim Abraham, had emigrated from Burma 42 years earlier. He spent his first four years in Israel living in a tin shack with dirt floors, but then the government sent him to cooking school. There was Eli, an assistant cook who had emigrated from Morocco, Sonia from Romania, and Joseph, Olga, and Moses who had emigrated from India.

As promised, Volunteers for Israel did offer us many lectures and trips. I heard lectures on the PLO, the Entebbe hijacking, Operation Solomon when 16,000 Ethiopian Jews were scooped up in the space of 36 hours and brought "home."

On the back of a military truck we were taken to Tiberius, a resort on the Sea of Galilee. We took a boat tour on the sea, and I found that some realities should be avoided. The cruise was a disco cruise and the young people danced to the music of Michael Jackson. On the shores of this sacred sea where Jesus himself walked on water were empty plastic bottles and litter. I wanted my Sunday school images back.

I didn't want to leave Israel after three short weeks so I volunteered to stay on for another three-week period. This time I was sent to a tiny camp of only seventy soldiers, a few miles from the Syrian border. We could hear the Syrian soldiers' guns go off and see puffs of smoke where the ammunition exploded. Here my main job was to weed a pathetic little garden planted in cracked, dry earth. I sensed right away that this was busy work to keep me, the older volunteer, occupied, but I didn't want to waste my time. I wormed my way back into kitchen duty.

I lived with seven volunteers in a hut with ants, mosquitoes, and creaky cots. The bathrooms were outside, 200 feet away, but we saw beautiful sunsets, had a breathtaking view of the distant mountain, and were fed very well. I could live with the inconveniences.

Our leader at this base was a 45-year-old reservist who took us to a Yemenite restaurant, for a nighttime swim in the Sea of Galilee, to a Druze (a Muslim sect) village, and for a really rugged four-hour trek through the Golan. The hike put one man in bed for two days, and a truck had to be sent for a woman who couldn't breathe. Another lady fell and cracked her head sliding off a rock. I fell, too, but only skinned my hand and my shin. We were in the sun for the whole hike, and it was at least 100 degrees. As we came out of the last ravine, an army truck was waiting next to the River Jordan with a complete chicken dinner. I was proud of myself, to say the least. I was the oldest in the group (although I told everyone that I was 55).

From this base, I took more trips sponsored by the Volunteers for Israel. I spent three days in Jerusalem in a soldier's hostel where I had to wear my uniform. I felt odd strolling through Jerusalem dressed as a soldier. I wasn't Jewish. I carried no weapons. In spite of the uniform, I would be completely useless in a crisis. If the truth be known, I was playing a game.

I went to the Wailing Wall which felt like a return to my days in Brooklyn with all the men looking like rabbis. I visited Hebrew University, the Billy Rose Sculpture Garden, the Yad Vashem Museum, the Knesset, the Chagall windows at the Hebrew Hospital and the museum that houses the Dead Sea Scrolls. I walked the path where Jesus trod on his way to crucifixion, the Via Della Rosa.

I also spent a weekend in Nazareth staying with the Sisters of Nazareth in their convent across from the Church of the Annunciation where Gabriel announced to Mary that she would have a child. I went to St. Joseph's Church above Joseph's carpenter shop, to Mary's well where she drew her water, and to the Church of the Adolescent Jesus. Nazareth is an Arab town, 50% Muslim, 50% Christian. On the Fourth of July I was at an Arab school high above Nazareth where 150 high school boys were studying English and algebra. I spoke to them at recess, and it seemed like each one had a relative in Chicago, Florida, or

San Diego.

I saw an interesting outdoor market snaking up the side of a hill where I could buy live chickens, every kind of fruit and vegetable, fresh eggs. In the middle of this stood a minaret bleating music five times per day, calling the Muslims to prayers. To my unaccustomed ears, the music sounded strange and eerie. I perched on a stone wall behind the goat cheese hawker and watched the Muslims kneeling on their rugs, moving up and down, and placing their foreheads to the ground in prayer.

I took the bus with other volunteers to the Amida Winery where I watched Israelis making pear wine and then to the Lebanese border to see the Arabs returning home after their day's work in Israel.

I also saw the beautiful Kibbutzim (collective farms) under the Golan Mountains where the Israelis grow apples, olives, oranges, and melons.

Our volunteer group always traveled with four armed soldiers who made sure we stayed together. The New Yorkers in our group said they felt safer here than on the New York subway.

I still wasn't ready to leave after this assignment so I signed up for another three-week stint. For this job, I traded in my army uniform for a hospital uniform. I was assigned to a hospital just outside Tel Aviv for developmentally retarded women. This was definitely a challenge for me. I was assigned a 60-year-old woman named Ruth whom I was to dress in the mornings, get ready for bed at night, pat dry after a shower. I even had to put her false teeth in a glass to soak overnight. I was also supposed to give her swimming lessons but she was spastic and could not even walk, so I was too nervous to take her swimming.

I quickly found out that I would have never made a good nurse. Dealing with a naked body and being surrounded by retarded women was very, very difficult for me. I stuck it out. But I did ask another volunteer to do the false teeth maneuver and to dress and undress Ruth. The best I could do for Ruth was to push her wheelchair down to a busy street so she could watch the traffic and people go by while I read a book.

When those three weeks came to a welcome close, I volunteered for my final stint. This time I was sent south to Ashqelon where the largest Israeli tank base is located. I was back in my army uniform, behind barbed wire, and escorted by armed soldiers. My job was to paint brake drums for the tanks and to sandblast carburetors. I was better with these hunks of machinery than I was with Ruth. From Ashqelon I was in striking distance of Beersheba, the Negev Desert, the Dead Sea, and the famous fortress of Masada.

One group of people I was anxious to meet personally was the Russian immigrants. I wondered how they were faring. I saw a Russian woman in a grocery store and said something innocuous like, "Oh, I like this neighborhood. Do you live near here?" That's all she needed to hear before I was engulfed in her life story and invited to her room in a hotel. She was very bitter. She was a high school teacher and her husband was a professor. They had been promised good jobs if they came to Israel.

"You see," she said as she pointed out their belongings piled in the corners of the small room and covered with bedspreads. "We have been here two years already and still we are in the same small room. They tell us we will get an apartment, but we wait and wait. They tell us we will get good work, but we wait and wait." I had to sit on the edge of their bed which completely filled the room because there was no place else to sit.

The Ethiopian Jews were not much happier. They came to Israel so quickly and in such large numbers when they were rescued in "Operation Solomon" that they had to be housed in thousands of small trailers set out on land with no shade trees.

Always at the back of my mind, I was trying to figure out if there was hope for peace in this region of the world. I asked the soldiers what they thought the future held. One conversation was frightening to the extreme. The soldier explained how one day the Jews would build their Third Temple and how crucial it was to them. I asked him where they were planning to build this temple. He said it would be built where the present Dome of the Rock stood. This Dome of the Rock is a very sacred building to the Muslims. The Dome had just been redone with a layer of pure gold paid for by the King of Jordan.

"Why don't you pick a different spot for your temple?" was my naive question. "Obviously, the only way you're going to get that spot is to demolish the Dome of the Rock."

"We don't pick the spot," came the reply. "God picks it."

My hope for peace in Israel began to disappear.

Many Israeli soldiers voiced the sentiment, "The only good Arab is a dead Arab." It was time for me to go over to the "enemy" and hear what they had to say about the Jews. Will you be surprised to learn that what I heard from the Arabs was "The only good Jew is a dead Jew"?

I got to be friends with two American women who were in Israel to work with the Palestinians, Sister Elaine Kelly and Mary Cook. I realized that they could help me get a job teaching in a Palestinian school. Like so many other places in the world, the Palestinian villages were desperate for English teachers.

Through Mary Cook, I lined up a six-month job teaching English conversation to Arab high-school students in the village of Kafr Kanna, also known as Cana, where Jesus had performed his first miracle of changing water into wine. Kafr Kanna was home to 11,000 Palestinians, 80% Muslim, 20% Christian. A minaret stands in the center of the town near two Christian churches, both claiming to be the site of Jesus' miracle. Thirty thousand tourists visit Kafr Kanna annually.

I was excruciatingly careful not to mention that I had just served in the Israeli Defense Force for three months. I knew that such information would turn every Palestinian in Kafr Kanna against me. When asked what I had been doing in Ashqelon or Jerusalem I would answer, "Visiting friends." It was a bit nerve-wracking.

I had wanted to stay in a hostel or rent a room, but was told, "That is not possible. It is against our tradition. You must live with a family. If you do not treat the house as if it is your own, we will be insulted." So I moved in with Hassan, his wife, Khaldye, and their three children, Dollal, Sane, and Thaer. They spoke almost no English. I had been told I would have a room to myself, but when I got there, I was instead pointed to a mattress on the floor in the girls' room. Neither Hassan nor Khaldye ever indicated what I could or could not eat so I didn't know if I should help myself or wait for a family meal. Bearing in mind that I was supposed to "treat the house as my own," I finally helped myself to pita bread and tomatoes. This became my standard meal while in Kafr Kanna. I was a little surprised at this treatment because I was told the village had been waiting eight months for an English teacher and that they were thrilled to have me. But I'm flexible, so I didn't let this put me off.

The house was bright and clean, but very shortly I developed ringworm on my back and chest—large, scaly disks of dried skin. An Arab doctor kindly treated me at no charge, saying I was helping the village so he would help me. At least someone appreciated my presence.

I was struck immediately by the contrast of life in Israel and life in Palestine. It felt like the Palestinians still lived as they did 1000 years ago, riding mules and keeping watch over their flocks. The streets of Kafr Kanna were full of potholes; the stores were dark and dingy. In some ways the comparison was unfair. I was comparing Kafr Kanna, a small town, to Tel Aviv, a cosmopolitan city. And I wondered how much of the differences were cultural and how much was due to the Israelis being the ones in power.

Mary Cook, who arranged my job, told me it was good that I was older because no one would bother me, but she was wrong. I could sense hostility as I walked around town. If I passed a group of young men, they would make a hissing sound. Or they would talk and then laugh, and it felt like it was directed at me. To the people of Kafr Kanna, Saddam Hussein was a hero and America was evil.

I was introduced to one middle-aged man and he replied, "Your president [George Bush Sr.] is murderer. He kill Arabs. You see that donkey? Bush worse than donkey!" Oh, nice to meet you, too.

Now I'm sure the Palestinians in the village had trouble dealing with my presence—a single American woman, walking freely around their town. Why wasn't I home attending to the needs of my husband and children and cooking dinner? I was an enigma to them, and I'm sure I made them very uncomfortable. Maybe the men were even afraid that their wives would get ideas.

On the other hand, I had some very entrancing experiences. On the night I arrived, I was taken to a wedding where 150 women were dancing in front of the bride to what sounded to my unaccustomed ears like one piercing and unchanging note. The groom and his friends were dancing at another house, and we didn't see them for three hours. As soon as I walked in to the party, all eyes turned from the bride to the foreigner. I was pulled onto the dance floor, touched, talked to, stared at, and told I had beautiful eyes. It was quite an ego trip.

Another time I was invited to my neighbor's house. She was 26 years old and expecting her sixth child. She hoped the baby would be a boy because she already had four daughters and only one son. She raised her eyes heavenward and said "Allah decides!" Half way through bitter Turkish coffee, she and her husband knelt on the floor, faced Mecca, bowed, and prayed.

My job was excruciatingly difficult. When I arrived at Kafr Kanna, I expected my classroom to be ready to go, stocked with dictionaries and workbooks. Hadn't they been waiting for a teacher for eight months? Instead, it was filled with a jumble of stacked furniture and supplies which I had to move out. Then I had to wash the desks and blackboard. I had no keys to my room and not one dictionary. Thankfully I had brought seven English as a Second Language books with me so I had a place to start.

I taught 47 students for two hours every afternoon. I was supposed to whip them into shape for the English portion of the entrance exams to university, but this seemed impossible. I looked over the exams and decided they would even be hard for an American student. Intricate reading comprehension sections on Bernard Baruch and Leonard Bernstein. Having lived all their lives in one Arab village, how could my students possibly relate?

And their skills were very weak. On one of my first days I asked an 18-year-old girl to count the numbers I had put on the board. When she got to 19, she looked confused. She continued, "Nineteen and one." On a quiz of the colors, one student spelled the words: brown—provon; purple—pvobol; yellow—yeluy; black—plake.

But far worse than their weak skills in English was the resistance I met. Correcting one student who said "He have," I said, "He *has*."

"Yes! I know. I forget!" he said in an annoyed tone of voice. It was all I could do not to say " For*got*!"

Another 18-year-old fellow said to me, "You learn me English. But no dictionary. I no like dictionary. You learn me how to pass exam!" Well, he was in luck. I didn't have a dictionary to unload on him. Frustration levels ran high, for me and for the students.

Of course, my students did make some progress, and I even became friendly with some of the girls. The boys were generally hostile, but some of the girls seemed to see me as a role model, inviting me home to meet their parents. One young woman walked me to her house, hair, neck, legs covered in wraps and robes. When we got home, she took it all off and there she stood—a totally new person.

Despite tiny victories like this, I soon realized I would not last six months in this job. I would be lucky if I made it to a month. I started to figure out when I would leave.

And then, it became clear to me that leaving Kafr Kanna was my *only* choice. I was walking back to my house around dusk. I was followed by a young boy, about 15, on his bicycle. He circled me and kept narrowing the circle. I wonder what he wants, I thought, as fear began to grip me. I told him politely that I was going back to my house with Hassan and Khaldye. I tried to explain that I lived with them. But he kept coming closer and closer till he finally lunged at me and grabbed my rear end. I yelled out to attract attention. He sped off on his bike. I ran back to my house and in a breathless voice explained what had just happened.

"We will find boy," Hassan assured me. "You come. Help find boy. We will beat him."

I knew in that instant that my work in Kafr Kanna was at an end. The hostility that I felt had erupted. What would happen next? Find myself in the trunk of somebody's car? No. I threw my belongings into my backpack, explained to Hassan and Khaldye that it wasn't safe for me to stay any longer. They thought I was overreacting. Maybe I was, but I just didn't feel safe.

As soon as I awoke the next morning, I hailed a cab on the main road to Nazareth. It was Shabbat so there were no busses going to Jerusalem. Instead I went to the Convent of the Sisters of Nazareth where they ran an immaculate hostel and I got myself a bed for $10. I tried to get my last week's pay from Mohammed Abbás, the man in Kafr Kanna who hired me, but he refused to send it to me. I knew he wanted to keep it for himself. Finally I met a wonderful Palestinian gentleman who called Mohammed and instructed him in no uncertain terms to meet him in Nazareth with the money. He did.

With my final wages in hand, I headed to Jerusalem to make plans to return home. I stayed at the Lutheran Hostel in the Old City of Jerusalem where 50 of us slept in what looked like catacombs. It was clean and safe and cheap, but I was told I could not stay there unless I was younger than 32. I was so angry I let the receptionist have it. "You mean to tell me that I, as a Lutheran, married to a Lutheran pastor, whose grandfather was the president of the Lutheran Church of America can't sleep in your crummy catacombs?" I had been pushed around enough in Kafr Kanna and wasn't going to take it now from the Lutherans. I was handed a key to a bed.

A few days later I was on a plane for New York and home, my three months in the Holy Land behind me.

eleven

Misadventures

But isn't traveling dangerous, especially for a woman alone? And at *your* age? I hear this question twice a week. People think there's a boogey-man out there waiting to trap innocent tourists. They see the world as sinister and think you have to be on your guard continually so that you don't get robbed, beaten, or snatched. My experiences in Kafr Kanna illustrate that there are some dangers to traveling. In my eighteen years of traveling alone, I have run into a few sticky situations and a few near misses. But they have been surprisingly few. With a little common sense, I have always been able to take care of myself.

There are always men who think that they are God's gift to the human race and can't fathom that any woman would reject them or simply not want to be bothered. After all, I'm traveling to see the sights, not to get caught up in some ego trip of a man I've never seen before. Who needs that? And yes, there does seem to be a disproportionate number of these men in Italy.

In Rome, an immaculately dressed fellow stepped up to me and said, "I'd like to take you on a tour of the city. I have my car right here." Short answer, "No, thank you." And, of course, I kept walking confidently ahead, never missing a beat with my steps. But he followed and said, "It won't cost you anything." Nothing, except possibly my life. I knew he spotted my passport and cash pouch hanging around my neck under my blouse. (I later switched to a money belt which can't be seen.) I looked like the perfect victim—American, female, alone—with a pouch around my neck. But I refused to be a victim. I kept walking straight ahead without the slightest hesitation until I disappeared into the crowd.

I never, ever get into a stranger's car. If I were to do that, I would give up all of my power to the driver. While I sat on a park bench on the outskirts of Rome, a man started up a conversation. It was all very pleasant and interesting. He invited me for a cup of coffee. I suggested the coffee shop across the street. No, he knew a much more interesting coffee shop. He could drive me there in a few minutes. End of conversation. Good-bye. If I had gone with him, they might have fished my body out of the Tiber River the next morning. He looked like the Ted Bundy type.

I have never had anything stolen in all my travels, but one time I inadvertently left my money belt on a toilet tank in the hostel in Edinburgh, Scotland. In it were my passport, debit card, cash, driver's license, phone card, Medicare card, and hostel membership card. In other words, my whole life. Forgetting all about my money belt, I walked out of the bathroom, out of the hostel, and I caught a bus to Glasgow.

Halfway to Glasgow something began to jog my brain. Something was wrong. What was it? And then in a terrible flash, I knew. I was not wearing my money belt. The image of it on the toilet tank appeared before me. It was all I could do to resist dashing up to the driver and demanding that I be let off the bus so I could run down the highway back to Edinburgh. No. Stay calm, I told myself. If I didn't get the money belt back, my trip was over. But I had left it in a women's bathroom, and women are trustworthy, I reasoned. I had a glimmer of hope.

Arriving in Glasgow, my heart in my throat, I hopped a cab to the hostel and explained the situation to the receptionist. He immediately got off a fax to the Edinburgh hostel asking if my money belt had been turned in. We waited five minutes before the fax machine started to spew out a reply. I was looking up to heaven with my fingers crossed. He was staring down at the machine. Suddenly I saw his thumbs-up gesture and he handed me the fax. It said, "Yes, we have Mrs. Jensen's money belt!" My trip would not end. My confidence in humanity soared. All was well with the world again.

I had another brush with danger on a train from Prague, Czech Republic to St. Petersburg, Russia. I left with great trepidation from Hlavní Nádrazí, the main train station in Prague, nervous about heading into Russia. The tales about the dangers of traveling in Russia were legion. I was constantly warned to be careful with my passport and money, to stay away from crowds, avoid gypsy families. If I were to take a taxi, I was told never to give the correct address of my destination. I should always pay in rubles because paying in dollars invited robbery.

The stories of train travel were even more terrifying. I had received many warnings about people being robbed in their compartments while they slept. So as I watched people board the train, I was relieved to see a father and his 12-year-old son come aboard and take the compartment next to mine. I needed allies and they were sure to be allies.

In the compartment on the other side of mine was a young, soft-spoken man wearing a saffron robe. I didn't notice his shaved head at first since he wore a hood. I made friends with him within minutes because I knew I needed him as another ally on this trip into the great unknown. He explained to me that he was a Hare Krishna monk from St. Petersburg. He spoke almost perfect English. After we chatted, he loaned me his tape recorder so I could listen to his chants. He shared his 400-page book of scripture about his Vedic faith. His presence made me feel much more comfortable as I headed into the Evil Empire.

I immediately mistrusted the Russian porter on our wagon. He looked like a prison warden with his big bunch of keys. He needed a shave. His shirt was dirty. He started getting drunk immediately. He epitomized what I had heard of chaotic Russian society. Any place that has been under Russian domination shows great physical deterioration, lack of goods, but worse, major trauma to the people. Russians seem lethargic, unimaginative, and zombie-like. I can understand why they seek refuge in vodka.

I spoke to my new friend, Jaraslov, the Hare Krishna monk, and explained my uneasiness.

"If I knock on the wall between our compartments will you come to help me?" He assured me that he would. I suspected that one of the keys on the porter's large key ring would open my compartment door from the outside.

I had two piles of cash, more than $700, stashed in my shoes and covered with two pairs of socks. Three hundred of this was from a friend in Boston who had given it to me to deliver to her cousin in Viljandi, Estonia. For her cousin, a medical doctor, this $300 represented a half-year's salary. These socks and shoes never left my feet. The money did get a big soggy, but it was intact. I didn't declare this money when the two tough customs women interrogated me in my compartment. If they had decided to strip-search me, I would have been in big trouble. Fortunately, my innocent face came through for me. I also had cash in three different pockets in my ski jacket which I did declare. My passport and Russian visa were in a pouch under my left armpit. I hoped everything was secure.

Then, of course, came the moment when the porter fell into my compartment dead drunk. I knocked on the wall and the monk rushed over to pick him up and send him on his way.

Suddenly the train schedule was changed. No, we're not going directly to St. Petersburg. We're going to cut off at Lithuania, go up through Latvia and Estonia and then over to St. Petersburg.

How can you simply change the route once the trip has started? I didn't bother asking because I knew I would get no explanation. My confidence in the Russian railroad system was fast eroding. My one-entry visa into Russia was now used up. Would I be charged an arm and a leg to get back in after going through the Baltic countries? No doubt I would, providing I would even be allowed back in.

My enthusiasm over my big adventure to Russia was fast diminishing. I didn't like this train anymore. It was time to make my exit.

When the train got to Vilnius, Lithuania, I grabbed my backpack, said goodbye to the monk, and made a dash for safety. I'd go to St. Petersburg another time. It had lost its allure. Instead I went to Estonia on local trains to deliver the $300. I was greeted like a hero. Much better.

Another danger in traveling I am particularly aware of is getting injured. An injury would not only end a trip, but perhaps my traveling lifestyle. I am always very careful. When I travel to countries where the traffic flows on the opposite side of the road from America, I never cross a street without first saying, "Look to the right. Look to the left for good measure. Now look to the right again." And I still keep my fingers crossed that I am not going to get run over by a taxi the way Winston Churchill did when he crossed a street in New York City.

In eighteen years of roaming around the world in every type of transportation and a lot on foot, I've had only one accident. I was walking down the main street in Glasgow, Scotland, when I suddenly was catapulted to the sidewalk. My fall came out of nowhere. Fortunately, I had my hands out of my pockets so I was able to absorb the worst of the fall with my hands and knees. Two men standing nearby lifted me up and asked if I was all right. All I wanted to know was "What happened?" I looked on the sidewalk for evidence of what could have done this to me. And there lay, so benignly, a loop of package strapping. This strapping, while made of plastic, is as strong as steel. I obviously had stepped on the loop with one foot and then put my other foot into the loop. Nothing was going to give except my body, and give it did.

I sat on a bench to assess the damage. Both knees were bleeding but nothing seemed to be broken. My hands had gravel stuck into the flesh. I realized quickly that I was very lucky. I had no broken teeth, no sprained ankle, no concussion. I sat for twenty minutes and thought about the randomness of life.

You might say I had a near-miss when the Swedish ferry, *Estonia*, sailing from Tallinn, Estonia to Stockholm, Sweden ran into a tragic disaster on September 28, 1994. The bow doors had not been closed properly, and during a fierce storm, the ferry was swamped drowning 847 people. I was scheduled on this same ferry two days earlier, but had changed my plans at the last minute. When I heard of the disaster, I immediately called my son in Los Angeles to tell him the comforting news that his mother had not been on that ferry. "What ferry are you talking about, Mom?" Oh, forget it.

Are there dangers out there? Yes. But I have avoided most of them with a little common sense and by listening carefully to my gut. Despite a few womanizing Italians, a misplaced loop of strapping, a ferry disaster that I was never a part of, and an aggressive adolescent in a Palestinian village, I still believe that the world is a gracious, safe, and remarkable place.

twelve

The Opiate of the Budget Traveler

A cornerstone in my approach to travel is the church. No, I am not a missionary or an evangelist. I just think that churches offer the best show in town: organ and choir music, richly outfitted priests, cute altar boys. And it's all free. You don't have to be a believer. Going to church is a perfect opportunity to experience a culture. Are the people old or young? What are they wearing? Is the church packed or half-empty? What kind of music is played? Do people talk to you, a stranger? I've attended services in German, Finnish, Chinese, Korean, and Spanish. I've been in the High Masses of the Anglican Church; the rocking services of black gospel churches; a church in China with 5,000 members; the sparsely attended service of a dying Lutheran church in my home neighborhood of Brooklyn, N.Y. I have been known to attend four different services on a Sunday morning.

I've even had two audiences with the pope. I am not a Catholic, but across the world I have seen the power of the Catholic faith and the love the people feel for the pope, so I wanted to attend one of his audiences.

I really didn't think that I could get in—me, in my slacks and running shoes, an obvious budget tourist and a Lutheran to boot. But I am not shy so I approached one of the Swiss guards in the Vatican and said, "I'd like to see the pope. How can I do it?"

He pointed up a stairway and said to talk to the priest in the second office on the left side of the hallway.

Heartened by his response, I flew up the steps and found the smiling priest.

"Hello, I'd like to see the pope."

"How many are there in your party?"

"Just one."

He handed me a ticket with the instructions to be at the Vatican one hour before eleven on Wednesday when the pope's weekly audience begins. I was in.

I was walking on air. I had to prepare myself for this visit. I had no dress or mantilla in my backpack. But I had to do something to get ready. All I could think of was washing the shoelaces in my running shoes. This simple act made me feel more worthy.

There were 5,000 people at the audience. A high school band from the Bronx, flamenco dancers from Spain, a choral group from France. People brought their gifts to the pope as the drummer boy brought his gift to the baby Jesus 2,000 years ago.

People were chanting "*Viva el Papa!*" The noise level was the same as at an Indiana basketball game. School children carried placards and waved them.

At the exact moment of 11 a.m., a door on the stage opened, bright lights came on, and out walked the pope in his white robe. It was pandemonium.

Pope John Paul II welcomed us in at least seven languages. He was kind and fatherly. The band from the Bronx played, the flamenco dancers danced, the French choir sang.

The priest in charge announced the pope would now bless the rosary beads, prayer books, or any religious artifacts we had brought along. I had two carved wooden angels to go over my grandson's crib. As I reached down to get them out of the bag, the priest assured us that it was not necessary to take anything out of bags. In fact, it wasn't necessary to hold the bags up. The papal blessing would go right through the bags, no matter where they were.

At the conclusion of the two hour audience, Pope John Paul

walked up the center aisle touching the visitors. Just behind him walked a photographer who clicked his camera every few seconds taking pictures of the pontiff touching the people.

I pushed myself toward the center aisle to have him touch me, but there were too many nuns in the way.

It was so easy getting a ticket to the pope's audience that I immediately decided to try for another ticket the next week to see if I couldn't get closer to the center aisle.

I got my ticket, went two hours earlier, and took up a position where I hoped I would be close enough for the pope to touch me. Sure enough, as he made his way down the center aisle again, he reached out and touched my hand.

That afternoon I returned to the Vatican to look at hundreds of pictures and found the one I wanted: Pope John Paul II with Dicky. Yes, I was glad that I had washed my shoelaces.

By far the most exciting religious event—and the most profound—I have seen was Holy Week in San Miguel de Allende, Mexico. There was drama, joy, music, and spectacle. I left San Miguel with my own religious beliefs in tatters.

I have always been a Lutheran. My grandfather was the president of the Lutheran Church in America, my father was a Lutheran pastor and preached on The Lutheran Hour, and my husband was a Lutheran pastor who started three new churches in New England where many people think Lutherans and Lithuanians are one and the same. I was a Sunday school teacher and choir director for over twenty years. I believed this was the *one true church* and that we had all the answers.

Then I went to San Miguel de Allende. I was there to study Spanish in a four-week course. I am just this side of hopeless when it comes to learning languages, but there is a beautiful school in San Miguel, Academia Hispano Americana. Taking a course was a good excuse to have another adventure.

The school was set in a lush garden with courtyards and hanging foliage, and it had excellent teachers. I attended classes for four hours every morning and had the afternoons free to explore the town, shop in the markets, and sit in the plaza. San Miguel has an open market where fruits and vegetables are sold for pennies, gift shops of Mexican crafts, an excellent public library with many English books (20% of the population are visiting Americans), *posadas* (hotels) where I could watch CNN in the lobby, and the endless picturesque scene of everyday Mexican life.

I lived with Mrs. Maruka DeSoto in her boarding house, a ten-minute walk from school. For only $9 a day, I lived in a clean if Spartan room and ate with ten other boarders at one round table. There was always bread, rice, honey, preserves, melon, papaya, mango, and on some days, white wine.

But it was the celebration of Lent that most enthralled me. I watched in awe as old, wrinkled women wearing black shawls prayed. It was their eyes that got me. They saw nothing around them but the statue of the Virgin Mary. They looked at her with complete confidence that she was listening to their prayers. Love and devotion shone from their eyes.

Wait a minute. I learned in confirmation class that there was no such thing as a saint, that praying to statues made of stone was a pure waste of time. But could I deny what I was seeing? What made me and the Lutherans right and all these people wrong?

As Lent progressed, I continued to question my beliefs:

I watched six-year-old altar boys who were barely old enough to ride a bike ringing bells and bringing various chalices to the priest at just the right time in the complicated service.

I saw hundreds of families with three, four and five well behaved children flocking to Mass.

I counted thirty-four—thirty-four!—huge bouquets of white chrysanthemums displayed on the three-tier altar in the cathedral, put there by believers to honor Jesus, his mother, and the saints.

By walking quickly, I attended four different jam-packed church services on a Sunday morning.

I was dazzled by the cathedral lit up at night, more impressive than Cinderella's Castle in Disney World.

The most moving sight I experienced was the Festival of the Virgin Guadalupe. The church dedicated to her was out in the country. I was sitting in an air-conditioned bus at a window-seat when we passed an endless stream of pilgrims whose destination was this church. It was very hot, dry, and dusty on the road. The pilgrims were carrying bedrolls, bags of oranges, and containers of water. Many were barefooted. Many had traveled for days, sleeping on the side of the road at night. They all had one goal: to pay homage to the Virgin of Guadalupe.

Could I possibly, in my arrogance, believe that I belonged to the one true church and that all these devout, believing people were wrong? No. On the contrary, I was humbled by such outpouring of love while under severe physical hardship.

In fact, I even mumbled a prayer to the Virgin of Guadalupe, although it was not a nice one. I looked up at the sky and said to her, "Don't you see these people trudging along a dusty road because they love you so much? Can't you come down from Heaven for just a moment or two, say 'Thank you,' and sprinkle a few drops of cool water on their hot foreheads?" There was no reply.

And then Holy Week arrived. At 5:30 on Palm Sunday morning, I went into the town to welcome the 5,000 pilgrims pouring in carrying statues of Jesus, Mary, and John. The townspeople had erected a mile's length of arches made of palms, flowers, and paper cutouts. Firecrackers went off constantly. Bonfires were lit.

On Good Friday, the entire town fell silent. Women wore their best black dresses and mantillas; the men looked somber in their black suits and white shirts. Not a sound was heard except for the mournful tolling of church bells. The streets were lined with thousands of people who neither moved nor made a sound. Then slowly, measured step by measured step, the procession carrying the dead Christ, his grieving mother and disciples moved through the streets of San Miguel de Allende. You could physically feel the love and devotion that poured from the hearts of the bystanders.

I left Mexico transformed. I had a new admiration for the Catholic faith and more questions about my own faith. But any trip that makes me look at the world with new eyes is a success.

thirteen

Don't Close the Door

I like to be where the action is. Czechoslovakia's Velvet
Revolution took place in 1989 so, of course, I was there less
than a year later. Czechoslovakia had been under Russian domination since 1948. It was considered one of the most repres-
sive countries in Eastern Europe. All internal political dissent was
stifled. In late 1989, however, a wave of democratization swept
through Eastern Europe with the encouragement of the leader of the
Soviet Union, Mikhail Gorbachev. Mass demonstrations broke out
on Wenceslaus Square in Prague. Václav Havel, the writer and dis-
sident, became the first president. With the end of communist rule
and the reemergence of democracy, the Velvet Revolution had suc-
ceeded. Not a shot had been fired.

I got a job teaching English to high school students at a hotel
school in the spa town, Karlovy Vary. I was the first and only
American in town. I spoke no Czech. It was the most demanding
and rewarding experience of my life. I had to call forth every skill
and bit of know-how I had learned in life to make it through—from
using Chanel #5 perfume and a toothbrush to clean my typewriter
keys to starting my own Berlin airlift to get the supplies for my
classroom.

In my quest for a teaching job, I first went to Prague. There I
saw Europe as it had been under the Hapsburg Empire. After 40
years of neglect under communism, the buildings were dilapidated,
but the old grandeur and beautiful baroque architecture shone

through. Wearing my Václav Havel button, I joined the crowds strolling down Wenceslaus Square where the Velvet Revolution started. Good King Wenceslaus looked out from astride his horse. In front of him were heaps of flowers laid down by the citizens of Czechoslovakia and a foot high ring of wax where the candles burned through the long nights of the Revolution. People had a gaiety about them, and the air was charged with newfound freedoms.

From the top of the hill where the Prague Castle stands, I could see our glorious American flag waving in the distance. The embassy. I immediately hotfooted it over there to let the staff know I was in town and to see if I could get a teaching job for next year. A handsome Marine in his dress blues sent me to the officer in charge of Press and Culture who sent me to Mrs. Stasa Zauitkouská at the Ministry of Education on Karmalitska Street who, in turn, sent me to a hiring agency located on a narrow street in the heart of Prague

Once there, it took exactly five minutes to get a job.

I stopped in at this dark, depressing agency that hires teachers and said, "I would like to teach English in your country for one school year."

The dour man nodded and said, "Wait. I come back in minute."

Sure enough, he came back from inside an even darker office and said, "You go here," pointing to an address on an index card.

It was a vocational hotel school in Karlovy Vary. He didn't ask if I had gone to school beyond the 6th grade, didn't ask for references or school transcripts, didn't know if I was a stable person or a fugitive from justice. Simply, "You go here."

The salary was $120 a month and included a free room on the fifth floor of the school and a 30 cent lunch each day. The experience would turn out to be priceless.

Karlovy Vary is the most beautiful town in Czechoslovakia. It has twelve natural hot springs that have special healing powers. If you drink from one it will cure your kidney stones. Another will help you get pregnant. Another is good for the heart; another for the circulation and on and on. Karlovy Vary is described as a "wedding cake" of a town, each building outdoing its neighbor in opulence, baroque trim, and exuberant statuary. It's as though one wandered on to a movie set. It sits in a valley surrounded by mountains with the Ohre River flowing through the center.

People from all over Europe come here for a three-week cure. To cater to these "patients" or guests, huge sanatoriums and hotels, restaurants and shops fill the town.

Some of the famous people who have visited Karlovy Vary are Chopin, Goethe, Schiller, Smetana, Dvorák, Beethoven, and the kings and queens of bygone empires. It was the jewel city that attracted the rich and famous.

I found my school, Strední Odborné Ucilsté, right in the center of town, housed in a beautiful baroque building. Right next door to the school was the *kino*, or movie theatre. On the other side of the school was the main post office where I could make international telephone calls. Across the street was the largest hotel, Thermal. Built by the communists, it was the ugliest building in town. Right in the vicinity of the school were grocery shops, clothing and shoe shops, and delicatessens.

Once I arrived at my school, my first stop was the principal's office. I introduced myself as the new English teacher.

Stares! Gasps! An American woman? How did she get here? I had sent a letter saying that I was coming on this date, but the principal didn't believe that an American teacher would actually show up. Because this was a vocational school, they didn't feel they were entitled to a real English-speaking teacher. The people in the office had heard all about America, but most had never seen a real live American before. That Velvet Revolution sure started something.

A group of high school students was quickly organized to empty a room on the fifth floor of the usual discards of a school: old cabinets, chairs, broken filing cabinets, newspapers, and school papers. They carried in a bed and desk, and I had a place to live.

At the other end of the hallway lived fifteen teenage boys who were boarding students. On the weekend they all went home and I had the whole building, five stories, to myself.

Since this was a hotel school the students studied one of three courses: Waiter and Waitress, Chef, or Butcher. One room was set up like a restaurant for the students to practice their waiting skills. Another room had charts of various cuts of meat and a replica of a pig that came apart. The cooking students were apprenticed out to the various hotels in town. These were four-year courses. It was with great pride that a student graduated as a waiter or a chef.

I was shown my classroom by the assistant principal. He spoke German. The crisis of language was averted as I had no intention of learning Czech. I could use my German and English. My old standby excuse when someone asked me why I didn't learn Czech was, "I'm not here to learn Czech. I'm here to teach English."

And then the work began.

When I saw my classroom I was duly impressed. It had lots of windows overlooking a park, a big blackboard with lots of chalk, and nice old-fashioned sturdy desks. I asked where the dictionaries and textbooks were kept, as there were none to be seen. The vice principal looked at me blankly. Dictionaries? No, no. Textbooks? No, no.

"We can buy in bookstore?" I asked.

"No, no. No English books."

Of course I didn't believe him and scoured every store that looked like it might sell books. He was right. No English books. No dictionaries.

My first challenge had arrived.

I turned the four walls of my classroom into a giant dictionary and textbook. From floor to ceiling I covered the walls with pictures of food, clothing, furniture, families, kitchen utensils, sports equipment, maps, and on and on. Wadded-up toilet paper became clouds on the weather chart; slivers of aluminum foil became rain. A half woman next to a half man was "divorce." I spent many evenings

110

pasting pictures on posters, printing out the words to songs, and figuring out how to explain various concepts.

And then I activated the Karlovy Vary Airlift.

The year before coming to Karlovy Vary, I had taught second grade in an American Department of Defense school in Butzbach, Germany. It was a school for the children of American military personnel who were stationed there. That school had everything a teacher's heart longed for: copy machines, tons of construction paper, encyclopedias and every conceivable workbook and textbook.

As I faced my empty classroom in Karlovy Vary, my greedy thoughts turned to the opulent American school six hours to the west. How could I transfer some of this wealth to my very needy school? It wouldn't be stealing. Many workbooks, half-used, were headed to recycling. Textbooks that were being replaced by more up-to-date ones were aimed at the dumpster. I didn't want new construction paper, just what was left over from a project and headed for the wastepaper basket. And old magazines that were being discarded had pictures I desperately needed to illustrate food, clothing, appliances, and furniture.

I sounded the Call to Arms. I have never met an American who wouldn't respond to a plea for help.

Packing up the trunks of their cars with my vital supplies, my teacher friends from Butzbach arrived after school on Friday to spend a weekend in Karlovy Vary. I put them up in empty beds on the 5th floor of my school. We drank Bohemian and Moravian wine, ate goulash, danced at the Hotel Pupp, shopped, met my students and fellow teachers, went to services at the incredibly beautiful Russian Orthodox church, St. Peter and Paul, and learned about life in Eastern Europe.

During the week before my American friends arrived, I shopped for the famous Bohemian crystal. When I spotted a good bargain in one of the state stores, I went into high gear. I bought twelve decanters in one afternoon, making four trips back to the store. I sent my friends back to Germany with their trunks filled with wine glasses, decanters, pitchers, fruit bowls, carafes, porcelain, champagne glasses, and chandeliers like the ones in the White House.

And my American friends had shopped for me. Someone had spread the word at the Butzbach School that I had lost weight, was not looking too good, and was eating poorly. My friends rushed to the PX and brought me vitamin pills, bananas, canned ham, enough Campbell soup to last three months, applesauce, 30 cans of tuna fish, smoked oysters, Oreos, Fig Newtons, and Twinkies. As if that wasn't enough, they also added the complete book of Beatles' songs for one of my students, two American calendars, two books of Christmas carols, a GI flashlight, shampoo, and hair conditioner.

I still needed encyclopedias but there wasn't one to be had within fifty miles. I casually mentioned to one of the teachers who had been an MP in the Air Force for 20 years, "I could sure use a set of encyclopedias. It wouldn't matter how old it was."

He quietly said, "You'll have your encyclopedias."

On the next trip over from Germany, an old set of encyclopedias was in the trunk of his car. The name of the school had been marked out with an indelible, black marker. They were on their way to the dumpster, anyway.

My airlift was every bit as successful as the one in Berlin.

The impact I made on the students that year was not so much in the English they learned but in their observing how a free American woman acts. Having been restrained by communism for 50 years, they had lost all spontaneity, creativity, and zest for life.

During the Cold War era, if someone laughed out loud on the street, it was reported to the police. So people blended into the woodwork, hoping not to be noticed. They stifled every natural expression.

How frustrating it was when I would explain a simple concept and be met with totally blank faces.

"Maybe I didn't explain it properly," I'd think to myself and explain it again.

Still no reaction.

"All right, I'll try again," I'd say to myself.

"No, no. Do not explain again. We understand," the students said in exasperation.

"You do? Well, I'm going to talk to this wall and you'll see that I get the exact same reaction from you as I do from this wall." I walked to the wall and talked to it very seriously—amongst titters from the students as they understood my point.

"Your faces are exactly like the wall. Nothing happens on your faces. It's like you are dead. I can't tell if you understand me or not."

"Yes," they would sadly admit, "we are stone faces."

That's what Communism did to its people.

I had to teach the students how to show their reactions, something that comes to Americans naturally.

"When I speak to you, nod your head to indicate you understand what I'm saying. All right. Everybody nod your head. Up and down, up and down."

"Now move the muscles in your cheeks. Get rid of your stone faces. Look alive."

"Now you have to learn to make sounds from your mouth. Ahhah, uhmmm, oooh, I see, hmmm, yes, mmmm . . . "

This might sound silly, but it was actually very difficult for them to learn. The students had to give it their full concentration. From being completely blank and silent, they had to use muscles they had not used before and make sounds they had never emitted. We had hilarious role-modeling sessions. I would make a remark about the weather to a student and he would shake his head up and down, make weird sounds, and work his cheek muscles in frenzy. The class would erupt in laughter. At one such eruption, the teacher in the next room tore open the door and looked at us with intense disapproval.

My next assault on the vestiges of communism was to show

my students that each of us has power to influence the government without getting thrown in jail. I told them I would write a letter to President George H.W. Bush, Ambassador Shirley Temple Black, and President Václav Havel. I was confident that each one would answer my letter, I explained, because I am an important person, a citizen, a human being. I have a voice. Of course, they didn't believe me.

The first response I received was from President Bush. When the envelope arrived in the school office with the words "The White House" embossed on it, a shock wave went through the office. One of the secretaries rushed it right to my classroom.

I acted completely nonchalant. "Well, of course, President Bush would answer my letter. That's not surprising. I'm a citizen of America. He works for me!" Huh?

We carefully opened the envelope and out came a Christmas card, a painting of the Oval Office. Inside were the words, "Barbara and I wish you and your students a very happy Christmas." It was signed by the president.

It was passed carefully around the room from one uncomprehending student to the next.

"We should be hearing from Shirley Temple Black and President Havel soon," I assured them.

Ambassador Shirley Temple Black not only wrote a friendly note in her own handwriting but she enclosed 200 stickers of the Czech and American flags intertwined to give to each student. That envelope with the address, American Embassy, Prague, also caused a major commotion.

President Havel, poor man, was so busy getting his country changed from communism to democracy that he had one of his staff respond to my request that he send me two dozen English dictionaries. This letter from the Palace in Prague stated that the President had much greater concerns at the moment than sending me dictionaries. "We are very sorry, but you will have to solve this problem yourself." Fair enough. I had made my point with my students that

114

someone, no less than the president of a country, would respond to a regular citizen.

There were more battles. People who have been under communism always close the door when they enter a room. It's a form of safety, I believe. No one can see who is in the room and report you to somebody. I never allowed a student who came into my dormitory room to close the door, but they automatically closed the door without fail. "Why do you keep your door open, Mrs. Jensen?" they asked.

"I have nothing to hide. I want to see who's going by my room so I can say hello. I want the students to feel free to come into my room and talk. *Don't close the door!*"

My classroom was also the only one where students' work was displayed. I innocently hung some student papers out in the hallway my first week in Karlovy Vary. When I came in the next day they were all gone. I finally found out the vice principal had taken them down, and I was told, "No, we don't do that." But over time it became apparent that the steamroller of American energy and principles could not be stopped. I was determined to bring a new spirit into the school, a spirit of fun and celebration. I knew teaching English was important. But what I felt was infinitely more important was to celebrate holidays, sing with gusto, tell other people you loved them. These were all foreign concepts to the Czech mind under communism.

Under communism, holidays were not celebrated. Christmas and Easter were ignored. People had never heard of St. Patrick's Day, Valentine's Day, or Mother's Day. I wanted to change all that. The first celebration was to be the 72nd birthday of Czechoslovakia on October 28. It's the same kind of holiday as our 4th of July. As far as I could determine, nobody was planning any kind of celebration. I would have lost my job if I didn't talk about July 4th in America.

As incredible as it might sound, mine was the only classroom that celebrated this important day. The rest of the school went about its usual business. I couldn't believe it. You might not celebrate your country's birthday, I thought, but, by Jiminy, my class sure will.

Across the front blackboard I wrote in large letters with different colored chalk, "HAPPY BIRTHDAY, CZECHOSLOVA-KIA!!!!!!"

I had my classes sing the birthday song many times, encouraging the students to sing as loud as they could in the hope that the sounds would filter down the hall. "Yoo-hoo, it's your country's birthday!" I was trying to say.

Each student made an elaborately decorated birthday card which was hung on the wall. The cards said Way to Go! Great Country!, I Love You, CSFR. The students brought candy to share and we blew up balloons. We played Elvis Presley songs to give the birthday party a festive mood. When Elvis sang "It's one for the money, two for the show," I reached for the hand of the class clown indicating I wanted to dance with him. He blanched. The students erupted in hysterics more from embarrassment than joy. Whoever heard of a teacher dancing with her students? It was culture shock time. But I felt it was important to show them that, yes, a teacher can have fun with her students. Some teachers drifted down to my room to see what was going on. We greeted them with "Happy Birthday, Czechoslovakia!"

It was a birthday party not soon forgotten.

The next holiday to come along was Thanksgiving. This is not a Czech holiday so school was in session as usual. But the American teachers in Germany had four and a half days off and wanted to spend them with me and my students in Karlovy Vary.

They came loaded down with a complete Thanksgiving meal. Two teachers sat in the back seat of one of the cars so tightly wedged in by food and supplies that they couldn't move an inch.

Among the supplies was a roasted turkey, a large Tupperware container of turkey gravy, a spiral-cut ham, vegetables, cranberry sauce, and all the trimmings.

This was too good an opportunity to expose the Czechs to an American holiday to let it slide by. We invited the fifteen teenage boys who lived at the other end of the hall to share in an American feast. We set the tables up at my end of the hall. We used paper plates and tablecloths the Americans had brought from the commissary. We lit candles and were ready to entertain.

Each boy was served one olive, one small cube of ham, three kernels of corn, four baked beans, a teaspoon of cranberry juice, and an Oreo. They said it was all delicious, but I'm sure they made a bee-line to their lunch of dumplings when their Thanksgiving feast was over. We basically wanted them to experience a happy, sharing atmosphere.

We sent word down to teachers to come on up and see what the crazy Americans were up to. To their menu we added a thimble-ful of vodka and orange juice.

It was an outstanding Thanksgiving. One student sent me a note: "We gratulation to your thanks given day!"

For Christmas I broke all the rules. The children performed. I interrupted the routine class work and took my class from class-room to classroom to sing "Jingle Bells" with real bells and "We Wish You a Merry Christmas." Both the audience and the performers felt embarrassed and awkward. I had to physically push the children into the classroom for their first performance. Then it got easier and easier.

In fact, they liked it so much that we ended up singing in the grocery store, in front of the *kino*, and at the Thermal Hotel. We still got uncomprehending stares from the passersby, their looks asking, "What kind of nonsense has the Velvet Revolution wrought?"

We decorated the windows with snowflakes, candy canes, and snowmen. It was sad to stand outside the school and look up at the windows and see that ours was the only classroom decorated for Christmas.

Earth Day, April 22, took off like a rocket into outer space. The ecology teacher, Blanka Silvanová, announced there would be a poster contest. First prize 300 Kc or $3, second prize 200 Kc, and third prize l00 Kc. Here was a chance to tap into the students' creativity and imagination that had been bottled up for so long.

When Mrs. Silvanová breathlessly came to me saying, "We have big action," I knew the poster contest had taken off. Before it was over, every wall going up five flights of stairs was covered with unbelievably creative posters. We turned many of them into placards and marched around town. People looked baffled. What is this, another Communist demonstration?

"No," we shouted, "Save our Earth." When you tap into creativity that has lain dormant for 50 years, anything can happen. And it sure did on Earth Day.

I had more tricks up my sleeve. We plastered the walls with hundreds of green shamrocks for St. Paddy's Day. "What those green things mean?" was the question of the day. The school looked like a "love-in" for Valentine's Day. Teachers received cards that said, "I love you" which left them nonplussed and self-conscious. For Mother's Day we made life-sized cutouts of mothers to hang in the hallways. They came in all shapes and outfits. We attached words "I love you, Mom," "You're the greatest, Mom," "Thanks, Mom!"

These were the high points, and of course, there were low points. Very low points. At times the stone faces just got to me. I was worn out from struggling for every little victory. I was driven crazy by my 14-year-old students and their crazy hormones. It annoyed me that when I wanted to use a public WC, I had to buy a 3-cent ticket from one attendant, show the ticket to another attendant as proof of payment and to receive my allotted piece of toilet paper.

But I was mostly frustrated by the terribly annoying communist mentality. A student could not give me a direct answer. He had to first discuss it with his neighbors, and after a consensus had been reached, he would venture an answer. This drove me crazy. I wanted an answer from the student I asked, not from a committee.

And then there were the students I took to a snack bar. I saw up close how difficult it was for people who have been under communism all of their lives to think for themselves. We got to the snack bar and the students asked me to ask the waitress if they could smoke. I pointed to the large ashtray in the middle of the table and said there was no doubt they could smoke. Why else was the ashtray there?

"No, please, would you ask the waitress just to make sure?"

"No, I will not ask. If I see an ashtray my brain makes the connection that it's okay to smoke. I don't have to double-check with anybody."

Do you know that these frightened boys would not smoke until they had asked the waitress if they could?

My biggest slump came during my third and fourth months in Karlovy Vary. The first two months were easy because everything was new and different and exciting and challenging. But that began to wear thin, and I was faced with day to day plain hard work. There were many times when I could have:

A. Committed murder

B. Committed suicide

C. Taken the next train out of town

I went through many phases. The angry phase: "Don't you know how lucky you are to have me here?" The resigned stage: "Students, in a living room, we have a couch, an armchair, and a coffee table." The euphoric stage where I was sure that my 220 students *loved* me.

But I stuck it out, knowing this is part of living in a different culture. Your mood goes down for a few days (or weeks, in this case), but it eventually rebounds. Things come back into perspective and life seems good again.

And of course, I had some fabulous experiences outside of the school to help me cope. One was at the Hotel Pupp, the oldest and most beautiful hotel in Karlovy Vary. (No matter how you pronounce Pupp, it comes out Poop.)

The master chef heard that there was an American in town teaching English at the hotel school where his apprentices were studying. He invited me to the hotel for dinner. Four waiters were lined up to greet me. Gorgeous Bohemian chandeliers shone from the ceiling. Fresh flowers were everywhere. The headwaiter wore a tuxedo with satin lapels. The other servers wore a red or white jacket depending on their job. The women wore black dresses with little white aprons.

The headwaiter ushered me to a table that was set with a wineglass, water goblet, exquisite porcelain, and sterling silver utensils. He said this table would always be waiting for me. He sold me special meal tickets that entitled me to a meal for 6 Kc or 15 cents.

"Would you like to start with an aperitif?" Sure, why not?
It was a special liqueur called Becherovka made only in Karlovy Vary. It came with a sprig of peppermint.

A dolly filled with appetizers was then wheeled in by Red Jacket. I picked a cheese wrapped in ham.

Then came a piping hot beef and vegetable soup. For the entrée, I was served a typical Czech meal: roast duck, creamed white cabbage, and dumplings washed down with a white wine from Moravia.

I couldn't believe what was happening to me. All that food, plus ambience, for 15 cents? It brought back memories of my youth in Brooklyn when I could buy a hot dog, a pretzel, and a mug of root beer for 5 cents.

I went back the next night. Yes, my table was waiting for me. They were delighted to see me again.

"Wouldn't you like a dry sherry to start?" Of course! It arrived in a frosted glass.

The dolly arrived and I picked out caviar and egg. The headwaiter suggested I have the beefsteak, four fresh vegetables, boiled potatoes, and a red wine. I saw White Jacket coming to my table with a gas stove. He poured several liqueurs on my steak and set it on fire. It was as tender as butter. With it I had breaded kohlrabi, creamed carrots, spinach, and tiny potatoes.

The simple reason why I was wined and dined so lavishly was because I spoke English and I was sharing that English with the future chefs, waiters, waitresses, and butchers of Czechoslovakia.

The evening I had the steak, I taught the waiter the difference between "This steak is tender," and "This steak is tough."

He came back in a few minutes with a big smile and said, "I understand. Like Elvis Presley—Love me Tender." Right on!

I couldn't keep up with such a rich diet, so many drinks, and the time it took to get dressed and then eat such a grand meal. After all, I still needed to be prepared and awake so I could teach my high school students for six hours the following day.

So, sadly, after a few weeks of living an opulent life style, I decided to return to being Cinderella before she married Prince Charming.

I had another interesting experience in Marianske Lazne, another spa town. To get there, I had to sit on a Toonerville Trolley that ran about ten miles an hour. It went through farm country, stopping at little villages where wooden sheds had been erected as train stations. The round trip, two hours each way, cost 30 cents.

As I was walking down the main street in Marianske Lazne, I saw a poster in a hotel window showing the American flag and the Czech flag. The poster went on to thank the American soldiers who freed this part of Czechoslovakia in 1945. I went into the hotel and had my $1.30 meal (turtle soup, sauerkraut, potatoes, baked pork roast, and a pot of tea). I asked the waiter if I could buy the poster. "I am from the U.S.A.," I explained.

"Please wait ten minutes. My chef (boss) talk with you."

Ten minutes later this plump, pleasant woman came to me with the poster. Of course, it was a gift. She told me she had an American Club in her hotel and would I like to see it. She took me upstairs, opened several doors, and we came to a very special room. On the walls were painted in large letters: The White House, Delaware, Texas, Nebrasca [sic], Virginia, etc. All over the walls hung American and Czech flags. Then she turned on the lights for the dance floor and they were red, white, and blue. I almost started singing, "Glory, glory Hallelujah!"

Then she told me that the president of the American-Czechoslovakian Club was in the hotel at this very moment and he would like to meet me. He couldn't speak a word of English so he just took my hand and kissed it.

She asked me if I would be so kind and send her a Book of Regulations. What? I eventually figured out that she wanted a cook book so she could make our American food.

These people have never been to America but their love and gratitude for our country is very touching.

I had another interesting Czech experience when my student, Jarislov Soukup, invited me to his village, Zlutice, 45 minutes from Karlovy Vary.

It was the day the 200-pound pig was to be slaughtered.

To keep my school clothes from getting pig-dirty, Mrs. Soukup provided me with Czech working clothes—an ugly patterned apron, a loose-fitting house dress in another ugly pattern, an ill-fitting sweater, and the ugliest pair of gray, pointed Russian shoes I had ever seen.

Don't tell me that clothes don't have an effect on you. I felt I had lost my identity. When I got back into my school clothes at the end of the day, I got my real self back.

The butcher arrived at 8 a.m. We had our first shot of vodka with him. We followed the butcher out to the backyard and watched him shoot the nail into the pig's head that ended his life. The butcher immediately stabbed the pig in the neck. Mr. Soukup caught the blood in a pan and set it aside to be used later for the blood wurst and red soup. I never ate either item again.

The pig was then dragged into a wooden bathtub, sprinkled with a powder that loosened his hair, and doused with hot water. Another shot of vodka.

Everyone started rubbing chains across his back or rubbing

him with their bare hands to get the hair off. He was then strung up off the ground on chains with his head hanging down. The butcher made a long incision lengthwise down the pig's abdomen. All his insides were removed.

Another shot of vodka. This time washed down with a beer.

The various parts were then put into big pots for cooking. Steam began to fill the kitchen.

The first delicacy to emerge was the pig's brains which were mixed with scrambled eggs and eaten on bread. I almost couldn't face this unusual dish, but then I remembered I was traveling the world for new experiences so ate my share.

The next shot of vodka was crucial.

Then the cooked pig's parts were dumped on to a big cutting board. We were all allowed to attack these parts and cut off whatever we wanted to dip in horseradish or mustard.

Meanwhile the intestines were cleaned out, the bladder emptied. The big vats of sausage meat made from cooked meat, much fat, barley, and spices were pumped into the intestines. The meat and sausages were wrapped in freezer paper into meal-sized portions and stacked into the freezer.

Celebration time. A shot of vodka washed down with a beer.

The next morning I went to Catholic Mass with the family. The church was completely torn apart. Piles of stone lay around in the churchyard near half-empty bags of cement and haphazardly stacked wooden timbers. To get in the front door you had to walk on a wooden plank. I mentioned to Mrs. Soukup how nice it was they were renovating the church.

She said, "Oh, it's been like this for 18 years."

When we got back home from church shortly after 10 a.m., we all had a shot of vodka. No wonder they drink. Nothing ever gets done. There's no future. You kill the pig to keep yourself alive, but for what?

I hoped the Velvet Revolution would soon start making changes in people's lives. I felt I had contributed to this process of change, at least with my own students. When I left, the students were getting comfortable with English, many of them speaking decently. But I had also introduced them to a new life style, a new way of thinking and relating. I planted a big piece of America in Karlovy Vary. And Karlovy Vary planted a big piece of itself in me.

I go back there every few years because it is one of my favorite cities in the world. I have instructed my daughter to spread some of my ashes there. Even in death I plan to be peripatetic: my son will take some of the ashes to Brooklyn, N.Y. where I grew up; and my other daughter will take the rest to New Hampshire.

fourteen

Taking Advantage of Friends and Relatives: Asia

I had just arrived in Beijing and was in the typical panic of arriving in a new city with strange sights and sounds. I knew no one in this teeming metropolis and felt very much on my own. My first move to ward off panic: change money so that I would not feel powerless. I stopped at a bank and got in the money-changing line.

I felt someone staring at me. Glancing at the next line, I saw a Chinese man, his eyes fixed on me.

Oh, no, I thought, a con-man. He wants something. Just ignore him.

He kept staring.

What does he want? I thought. My heart pounded.

The man left his line and came straight for me with his hand extended. Here he comes, I thought and really started to panic.

But then he said the magic word: "Dicky!"

The memories flooded back. I cried out in recognition, "Tang!"

When I was 53, I had gone back to school at the University of New Hampshire for a master's degree in education and counseling. I was newly divorced and looking for direction. My daughter and I moved into university housing for students with families, a complex of 250 units located in a quiet corner of the campus. Keyun Tang lived in the same complex with his wife, Ping-Ping, and their two children. He was working on a doctorate in space physics. I often invited Tang and his family to my apartment to experience American food and hospitality, and he invited me and my daughter over to his apartment to experience Chinese food and hospitality.

Now, twelve years later, in a country of one billion, in a city of twelve million people, Dicky and Tang decided to change money on the exact same day, at the exact same hour, in the exact same bank. A billion to one shot.

With Tang by my side, I knew my trip to Beijing would now be a success. He would help me negotiate all the complexities of this beguiling city. More importantly, he would be able to show me a side of Chinese life that most tourists miss. I was certainly going to enjoy the gift of this lucky meeting.

As soon as we had our money-changing chore out of the way, he took me to an obscure restaurant down a side alley, a restaurant I never would have ventured in alone. The specialty seemed to be chicken feet; they were hanging by the dozens in the restaurant window. We also ate soggy dumplings covered with a white slime swimming in dishwater. Not every cultural experience is wonderful. Over dinner we caught up on our news. Tang and Ping-Ping were now divorced. As the eldest son in his family, he was obliged to return to China to look after his aging parents. Ping-Ping liked life in America and refused to return. Tang had remarried. His new wife was Lee, a doctor doing research in Chinese medicine. His children were in college in America and visited their father during vacations. After dinner he walked me down the Street of Night Food where a hundred vendors were dishing up more unfathomable foods like purple rice with hard peas, squishy fish balls, and pigeon eggs. These vendors set up their stands each evening, cooked and sold their specialties for a few hours, and then dismantled everything and went home.

He took me to the theatre where just buying a ticket is a very complicated procedure. He showed me the Summer Palace. He gave me a medallion from the Chinese Academy of Science. And most interesting of all, he took me to see his apartment. It was in a two-year-old high-rise. Even though he lived on the 5th floor, there was no elevator. The stairways were dank and dirty. But what really struck my Western eye was how the grounds around this new construction site were totally ignored. The leftover cement and bricks were strewn about. Piles of dirt and gravel stood where they were last used. The worn-out machinery and tools sat rusting. No trees or shrubs were planted, no sidewalks laid. Since this was public property no one was interested in it. It had nothing to do with the individual so it was simply ignored. It was as if it didn't exist.

One evening Tang and his wife, Lee, took me to a restaurant started by the victims of the Cultural Revolution. Lee's father, a professor, had been killed by the Red Guards. On the walls of the restaurant hung paraphernalia from that era: tin wash basins, Mao's *Little Red Book*, ears of corn, old jackets, and photos. We dined on a fish that was in the shape of an ear of corn!

As I left Beijing, I thought again of how important it is to take advantage of any and all contacts when you travel. I had seen things in Beijing I would not have seen on a tour. Some of it was not pretty, but I had a much better sense of China than if I had only seen its polished tourist side. And none of this would have been possible if I had not had Tang to show it to me.

Jang-Bal Ryu and his wife, Yoon, were two other friends I made in my days in family housing at the University of New Hampshire. Jang-Bal was working for his doctorate in forestry so he could return to Korea and help bring back the forests which had been destroyed during the Japanese occupation and the Korean War. I taught Jang-Bal how to drive a car, and I taught Yoon how to cross-country ski. They taught me to enjoy kimchi, the spicy national food of Korea. On graduation day, Jang-Bal received his doctorate in forestry and I received my masters in education. The Ryu's left for Korea and I went off to work for Aetna Life & Casualty. We didn't see each other again for ten years.

But while I was on a trip to Kumamoto, Japan, I realized that Korea was only a few hours away by hydrofoil. Not letting the opportunity pass me by, I wrote to Jang-Bal and Yoon asking if they remembered their neighbor from the University of New Hampshire and could I visit. Now, to some this may seem rude—essentially inviting myself for a visit— but I find most people are thrilled to have visitors, especially if they are from another country. So I was not surprised when I got a letter by return mail saying, "Of course we remember you! Of course you can come stay with us. It will be wonderful to see you again." The next week, I was off to Taegu, Korea where Jang-Bal was a professor at Taegu University.

Once I got to Taegu, new doors opened. The university was on its three-month winter break, and Jang-Bal asked if I would be interested in teaching English to seven professors during their vacation. Each of them had a doctorate and had studied English for ten years. What could I possibly add to their knowledge of English? I asked myself. But what the heck, I thought. I'll give it a go.

The first morning I walked nervously into the room where they were all sitting on the floor and said, "Oh, it's really warm out today." They looked at me registering absolutely no comprehension. I repeated, "It's very warm out today." Still nothing.

I put my hand to my forehead, rubbed it across, and shook it out as if shaking off perspiration. I said for the third time, "Very warm today." A glimmer of recognition.

"Oh, yes, warm, very warm. Yes, understand." I knew at that moment that I could teach them plenty.

Their names were Han-Bei, Yong Moon, Han Gyu, Koo Yeon, Hyuk Jin, Min Chul, and Jun Hyuk. I couldn't handle this. My weak ability in foreign languages meant I would never get the pronunciation right and I'd never remember who was who. I could easily waste a good chunk of the lesson stumbling over names. So I renamed them Tom, Mike, John, Bill, Bob, Harry, and Andrew.

Over the next weeks, the professors learned to tune into my American English. They slowly lost their terrible shyness and began to speak. Since then, Mike has spent a year at the University of California at Davis, Tom went to Syracuse, Bill attended Drexel in

Philadelphia, Andrew went to Johns Hopkins, and John is at the University of Georgia.

A few years ago we had a great get-together. I waited for a $100 air courier trip to Seoul and met my former students in the private room of an elegant Korean restaurant. I toasted them as the best English students in the world. They toasted me as the best English teacher in the world. After a six course meal we went to a Karaoke Bar and sang, "Oh, give me a Home," "Danny Boy," and "Let Me Call You Sweetheart."

While visiting Jang-Bal, I also experienced Cleaning Tombs Day. In Korea, bodies are buried in a softly rounded mound of earth covered with grass. A good tomb must have a view of the mountains and be near a body of water. If the tomb is positioned correctly, it ensures the offspring a good, long life with a good job and good salary. To get to Jang-Bal's parents' tomb, we drove down a narrow dirt road past rice paddies and then walked up a steep ascent to a clearing where a single, solitary mound stood. Although Jang-Bal's parents have been dead for thirty years, he visits their tomb four times each year.

As we approached the tomb, Jang-Bal laid out a mat. He poured out two glasses of rice wine and peeled two apples and a Korean pear, all of which were placed on the mat. Jang-Bal spoke reverently to his parents: "We are happy that the beautiful lady with the yellow hair came across the Pacific Ocean to visit you." He explained to me, "My parents had heard about America, but they have never seen an American until today. They are very happy that the 'delegation' came from America to honor their tomb."

Jang-Bal and his family bowed to the mound three times, poured the rice wine around the mound, and then we all ate the fruit. It was very moving.

After this ceremony we pruned the tall trees that were obstructing the view of the mountains. We cut the grass with scythes, pulled weeds, and raked.

Jang-Bal also took me along for the walnut harvest. Ten years ago he planted six hundred walnut trees; four hundred have survived. We were up at 6:30 and headed for his walnut farm which was two and a half hours away. We drove back into the beautiful mountains of Korea where the villages still look like they did a hundred years ago. The homes were made of clay and mud, and I could see an occasional cow in a barnyard. We drove down a very narrow road, parked the car in front of an ancient farmhouse, and walked half a mile up a steep hill to the walnut trees. Jang-Bal's relatives were already there to help with the harvest. The 73-year-old brother-in-law whacked the walnuts down with a long bamboo pole; his 66-year-old wife and I picked up the fruit. We did this all day long, just taking time out to eat a meal of rice, vegetables, and kimchi.

This venture in Korea illustrates again the wisdom of relying on old friends.

fifteen

An Experiment with Settling Down

I once tried to give up my traveling lifestyle. My friends, trying to give me advice, said, "Go find yourself a nice apartment in Boston. That's a nice city. You like Boston, right?" My brother thought I should settle near a good analyst and straighten myself out. My children said, "We want to know where you are so we can call you every Sunday evening to make sure you're okay." So although the thought of renting an apartment terrified me, I decided to prove to my kids, to my brother, and to the world that I really wasn't so weird. I would show them that I could live just like other people, that I could be normal.

I rented an apartment six houses down the street from my younger sister who lives in Rochester, Michigan. Her husband found a secondhand car for me so I could get to work. I landed a job as a temp worker at General Motors.

The apartment was downstairs from a lovely Lutheran family. The neighborhood had meticulously cared for houses and beautiful landscaping. Sprinklers ran in the summer evenings. People said hello to you as you took a stroll. It was the perfect place to try this experiment of settling down to "real life."

And it was a disaster. I refused to turn on the stove. I never put food in the refrigerator. I felt my life shrivel up every time I stepped into my apartment. Like my apartment in Durham, it was another tomb, but this time it was filled with secondhand furniture.

Within six weeks I said to myself, "Forget it. I'm not staying trapped in here, trapped in a boring job, trapped in a boring city. Sorry kids, you can't call me up every Sunday evening to see how my life in the tomb is going. I don't need to see a therapist; I need to see the world."

I called up the Cunard Line to see when the QE2 was next sailing from New York City to Southampton. It was scheduled to sail out the following week. I immediately made a reservation for a cabin on the lowest and cheapest deck. I could feel my spirits begin to soar. I was going to leave this dull, predictable world behind. I was going back to my exciting, unpredictable world. And the sailing would coincide with Thanksgiving Day, which was a great relief as I wouldn't have to shop for cranberry sauce and make gravy with the rest of America's housewives.

When I got to the Greyhound terminal in downtown Detroit to catch my bus for New York City, the QE2, and freedom, I was beside myself with happiness. When the bus appeared with "New York City" blazed across the top, I reached over and touched it and said, "Oh, thank you, bus. You're going to take me away from this awful place and bring me to New York and my ship so I can sail off for England. I'll be somebody again. I don't care if my friends think I'm weird. I'm not selling myself out to a dead-end life."

"But isn't it frightening to simply sail off for England or Portugal or Rotterdam?" I'm asked. "Where are you going to stay when you disembark from the ship?"

That's the easy and exciting part. To find a hostel or a B&B somewhere in Southampton or on up to London is exactly what living is all about. It's the need to be creative, to thrive. I have to solve problems on an hourly basis. What bus do I take to get from A to B? Where shall I have lunch? What's there to see? I am constantly affirming my creativity and potency. In the apartment I had no reason to stay alive because all my problems were solved.

I decided to live for a time in Marburg, Germany. I had been there once before and fell in love with the lovely castle sitting on a hilltop, the outdoor cafes, the bustling crowds, and the sausages in the butcher shop windows. I knew no one in Marburg. I had no contacts or letters of introduction. But I have learned never to try to figure out what I am going to do in a particular town or country until I get there. I knew I wanted to live in Marburg so I went.

That uncertainty gets my juices flowing. It's the opposite of living in an apartment where each day the big job is to straighten out the kitchen towels. No, life is now serious. I have to sleep somewhere tonight, and it's not going to be in a railroad station. I have to find food. The Kroger's super-duper grocery store, where an entire aisle is devoted to nothing but cereals, is now history. Every nerve-ending is on fire. My brain and body go into overdrive, which is exactly why I set off on this journey.

I met Irmgard Michel on the train going to Marburg because, of course, I was traveling alone. Our conversation started out with the usual, "Where are you from? What are you doing here?"

I said, "I'm an American and I want to live in Marburg."

She asked, "And why do you want to live in Marburg?"

"I was here five years ago and I loved it."

"And where will you be living?" she asked.

"Oh, I have to figure that out. I don't know yet."

Later, when we became good friends, Irmgard told me she said to herself, "*Ach, mein Gott.* What is this woman doing thinking she's going to come to Marburg and find a place to live?" But she could tell that I was a nice person, so she said, "Well, my husband is going to meet me at the train station and we would be happy to take you to some cheap hotel." She had seen my backpack. "And maybe we could help you find something more permanent." There it was. I arrived at my destination with my first night's lodging worked out and someone looking for an apartment for me.

The next day I put my ace-in-the-hole plan into action, in case my friend on the train didn't come through. I went to St. Elizabeth *Lutherische Kirche* (Lutheran Church) to ask where the parsonage was so I could speak to the pastor or, better yet, his wife. Because of my Lutheran background, I knew they would help me. I found the pastor's wife at the parsonage and introduced myself. "I'm a Lutheran pastor's widow from America." (I didn't want to get into the whole divorce spiel.) "I would like to live in Marburg, and I was wondering if maybe someone in your congregation would like to rent me a room or an apartment."

She looked at me as if to say, "*What*? Now I've heard everything!" But of course she said, "*Ja, Ja*. I'll be happy to help you."

In the meantime, Irmgard found me a great apartment. She was a lawyer and the judge she worked with had a mother-in-law suite. Since the mother-in-law had just died, he wondered if the American lady would like to rent that apartment for $200 a month. It had a picture window, a beautiful kitchen, living room, bedroom, and bath. There was bedding and every utensil known to a German kitchen including a potato ricer. The apartment was in a lovely upscale neighborhood.

Yes, the American lady would *love* to rent the apartment.

My four months in Marburg in my beautiful apartment were an unqualified success. Every Sunday morning the bells of St. Elizabeth Church rang out summoning me to the service. I attended organ recitals, joined the ladies' hiking club, had a real German Christmas complete with caroling and *Glühwein*, and made many new friends.

Why could I settle down in Marburg but not Rochester? That's a good question. Somehow, if I live in a different culture, I feel more alive. I am not living the same old routine I have lived for sixty years. And my stay in Marburg didn't feel permanent. It was not the end of my life but a temporary layover. At the end of four months, I moved on, bidding my friends good-bye, setting out for my next destination.

So is it nerve-wracking to board a train or a boat for a new place with little idea of what to expect? Yes, sometimes it is, but I feel it's healthy to be nervous and under stress at times. Then there is that surge of relief when I do find a bed in a hostel. Or the bus actually shows up and delivers me to the right place. If all events and outcomes are assured, as they were in Rochester, there is no thrill. I'd rather live life on the edge. Push the envelope. Don't play it safe. Play it risky. I have nothing to lose but security, and security is not what it's cracked up to be.

Do I want to go to my grave in an expensive box knowing I played it safe? Not when I could be saying, "I did it all. I lived life to the fullest."

sixteen

The Right Place at the Right Time

People talk as if it is lucky to be in the right place at the right time. I don't trust to luck. I put myself in the right place. For example, I was in Ireland when President Clinton made his historic visit to Dublin. I was staying in a hostel in Killarney, but as soon as I heard that he and Hillary were going to arrive in Dublin in a few days, I checked out of my hostel and hopped on a bus. I had to be there to see how the Irish would welcome my president.

All stores and businesses were closed for the day. The city came to a complete stand-still. At nine in the morning I was in front of the stage where he would speak at two o'clock. But as the mobs kept coming and pushing, I found myself in a crush, unable to move. I wasn't about to die in Dublin, so I wormed my way out through people 50 deep, shouting "Let me through, folks! An American coming through!" I saw Clinton's cavalcade go by and then made a brilliant move. I took a ringside seat at Daniel O'Connell's Pub where I watched the whole afternoon's proceedings on TV while drinking a pint of Guinness. One-hundred thousand people wildly waved flags and cheered this down-to-earth man who spoke right to their needs. Clinton was made a Freeman of Dublin, sharing the honor with Ulysses S. Grant and John F. Kennedy. "The Eagle has Landed" proclaimed the headline of one newspaper. It was a great day to be an American.

Again seeking out the right place, I went on a pilgrimage to England to bid farewell to Princess Diana after her death in 1997. I visited Kensington Palace where she had lived. There were fresh flowers at the gate, with more arriving every few minutes from people who still could not comprehend the great tragedy of her death. I went to St. Paul's Cathedral where the fairytale wedding took place and to Westminster Abby where the world said farewell. Finally, I went to Althorp, Diana's childhood home and last resting place. I drove slowly around the estate. I visited Great Brington, the neighboring town where all the Spencers are buried. Diana was to be buried there also, but the townspeople prevailed on her brother not to bury her there because the village was not equipped to handle the endless tour buses and tourists who would inevitably come. I went to the one pub in town, the Fox and Hounds, and raised my glass in a final farewell to Diana, Princess of Wales.

I was in Hong Kong in 1997 for this city's historic turnover to Mother China. Staying at a hostel in Kowloon, I was in the right place to witness this momentous event. Every skyscraper was covered with lights in the shape of Hong Kong's official flower and was festooned with slogans like "Back to Mother China." The longest dragon ever constructed—seven miles long and made entirely of lights—wended its way up Nathan Road. Prince Charles on the Royal Yacht, the Britannia, sailed into Hong Kong Harbor. Secretary of State, Madeline Albright, arrived as did Jiang Zemin, the president of China, setting his foot in Hong Kong for the first time.

A few days before the final turn-over took place, the British held their last farewell at a huge sports stadium. I pleaded with the officer at the Prince of Wales barracks to please give me one, only one, ticket to this last band and drum concert. He couldn't resist my pleas so I was able to join the thirty-thousand people crammed in the stadium in the rain, crying while they sang "God Save the Queen." The British flag slowly came down and was presented to Governor Chris Patton, the last British governor of Hong Kong. Off

138

in the distance, a lone bagpiper played a mournful tune. An era came to a close.

On midnight, June 30, the Chinese army trucks began to cross the border into Hong Kong. A dozen or so soldiers stood on the back of each truck. I had to look twice. Were they mannequins or human beings? Each soldier was positioned exactly as the next, his arm leaning against his body at the exact same angle as every other arm. They had absolutely no expression on their faces. It was eerie.

The next morning I visited the Prince of Wales barracks, now manned by the Chinese. The soldiers on guard never flicked a muscle. A few freewheeling Westerners tried to get them to smile or pose for a picture, but they may as well have been talking to the Great Wall of China.

My most exciting witnessing of history, though, was when I was in Berlin when the Wall came down.

I never thought I would see the Wall come down in my lifetime, even though President Reagan issued his order, "Mr. Gorbachev, take down this wall!" I was teaching school at the army base in Butzbach, Germany when I saw the headlines. The Wall was down!

This was an event I was not going to miss. I asked my principal for a personal day. With this day and the weekend, I had three days to be part of this historic event. I hopped a train on Thursday night in Butzbach and arrived seven hours later in West Berlin.

The first day I took a bus tour which took me to the Potsdam Crossing where the Wall was open. I went up to the Wall with my trusty Swiss army knife and hacked myself off a big bag full of graffitied concrete.

Over a million people from East Berlin poured into West Berlin that weekend. It was the first time they had been allowed to cross the border in twenty-eight years. The first thing the East Germans did upon crossing was to go to a bank where they could pick up 100 DM as a gift from the West German government. The second thing they did was to buy bananas which had been denied them all those years. Every trash can in Berlin was overflowing with banana peels.

The East Germans were easy to spot. They wore clothes about two notches below K-Mart. They had a tentative look about them, as if they were just emerging from a dream. They moved slowly, clutching their plastic shopping bags, as they tried to absorb all the new sights. Their hair was lifeless, their teeth were bad. In contrast, West Berlin was light and alive, the people moving with a brisk step; beautiful cars and motorcycles lined the streets. The East Germans had never seen anything like it. For those twenty-eight years, there had been no united Berlin, only East and West. They had lived in the Twilight Zone.

There were hundreds of TV vans at the Brandenburg Gate waiting for this crucial spot to open. There were also many white crosses erected there to commemorate the people who tried to make a break for freedom over the Wall but were shot in the attempt. Over 190 people died this way.

I was stuck at the famous Check Point Charlie for 45 minutes and watched the hordes of people showing their passports to the guards. Suddenly the guards were friendly and civilized. Last time I had been in Berlin, they wouldn't give me the time of day. Now they actually said, "*Guten Tag.*" I asked a guard in the train where the *Speisewagen* (dining car) was. After he told me, he said, "*Guten Appetit!*" What? Are you actually a human being?

I met two brothers from Atlanta, Georgia, who, when they saw the news of the Wall opening up, took the next plane out to be part of the celebration. They understood how easy it is to be at the right place at the right time. They kept calling to the guards, "Hey, *amigo*, say cheese!" Typically American. The guards were very uncomfortable with their new role. They couldn't quite bring themselves to wave to anyone and only managed anemic smiles.

It was wonderful to see the East Germans as they began to come back to life, but I had to ask, "Why were these people kept isolated all these years?" And that eternal question, "What is the point of man's inhumanity to man?"

After my weekend in Berlin, I headed back to my job in Butzbach, having once again been a small part of history.

seventeen

An Homage to JFK

I joined the Peace Corps for a very simple reason. I loved John F. Kennedy. I made a pilgrimage to Hyannisport on a Sunday morning to watch him going to Mass at St. Francis Xavier Church, waiting in the hot sun till he reemerged. He was so much bigger than life.

When he was assassinated, my world stopped. I loved his sense of humor, his boyish good looks.

Thirty years later, I wanted to honor him by joining the Peace Corps. At the time, I was 68. Would they take me? I filled out numerous applications, went through the medical exams, lined up references, and wrote essays. When I was accepted and received my assignment to the Czech Republic, I said to myself, "This one's for you, Mr. President." It turned out to be a less than perfect honoring of JFK's memory.

My first stop was Philadelphia where I met the other 28 people in Group V, as we were now known. We spent three days in Philly getting oriented to our task and getting to know each other.

Of the twenty-eight in our group, twenty were English teachers and eight were environmentalists. Eight had doctorates and our ages ranged from twenty-two to sixty-eight. I was the oldest but I like to believe that no one caught on, thanks to L'Oreal hair dye and good genes. There were four homosexuals who came out during the staging phase in Philadelphia. One, Bob from Boston, had been in the Peace Corps thirty years previously and had been dismissed when he said he was gay. In our new accepting environment, he was welcomed.

We lost our first volunteer after 48 hours. We lost the next volunteers two weeks later, after we arrived in the Czech Republic. By the end of the two years, 20% of group V would choose ET, or Early Termination, including me.

The training started in earnest after we arrived in the Czech Republic. We were sent to the hot spring town of Podebrady, one hour from Prague. It's famous for curing heart ailments. An ornate colonnade, surrounded by gardens, white benches, and statuary, sat in the middle of town for tourists and patients to stroll through.

We each lived with a host family to learn the language and culture. My host family consisted of Vera and Jirka Sykorová, their nine-year-old son, and the *babicka* (grandmother). I had a private room with a feather bed, piano, desk, and all the dumplings I could eat. My letters to all the folks who wrote references for me were ebullient: "Here is my first report to you wonderful people who wrote references for me which convinced the Peace Corps they couldn't get along without me. It's one of the best things to have happened to me and I will be grateful to you forever…. Being under the umbrella of the Peace Corps is even better than I had dreamed." The fly in the ointment was that I had to learn the Czech language. Czech is an inflective language with seven cases. What does that mean?

"Well," said the humorless Czech teacher. "Dis is Genitive Akusitam. You muss say Praze." Huh?

I finally figured out that depending on how a word like "Prague" is used, it becomes Praze, Prahou, Pragodech, Pragblahblahblah. I was in over my head.

The scientific finding on learning a new language is that the window of opportunity begins to close after age seven and is pretty well shut by the teenage years. My window was shut, locked, and double bolted. My attempts to learn French, Creole, and Spanish had taught me that.

We were on a fast track university schedule. Language classes were held five hours each day with three or four students per class and a professional teacher, so I couldn't bluff my way through.

Before long I was shifted to a class with three other male volunteers who were even dumber than I was. We called ourselves the "Special Ed" class, or the *Pomolous*, meaning "slow" in Czech. I learned to read most signs in town, read a menu, buy a train ticket, and ask for a single room with a bath down the hall. But I could never handle a political, religious, or current events conversation. No matter, I told myself. I had other sterling qualities.

These qualities showed up quickly when I did my practice teaching for two weeks in a local school. My Peace Corps partner, Jan, and I brought the students and the room to life with great animated activities. We set up a still life of a flower arrangement in a crystal vase placed on a colorful cloth, and we all set feverishly to drawing. Then we auctioned the masterpieces off. The pictures were so good, a bidding frenzy ensued. I wanted the one that looked like a Picasso. The teacher's pet wanted my picture. All sense of embarrassment or shyness—particularly debilitating in countries recently freed from Communist rule—flew out the window.

One morning, Jan came limping into the classroom on crutches and with a big bandage around her head. "What happened?" I cried out in mock surprise. She described her encounter with a car, what the police said, her visit to the doctor's office, and what her injuries were. The students then had to role-play a similar experience. Perfect lesson.

The evaluation by the assistant director confirmed my thoughts. "Excellent lesson; superb response. You keep the class with you. Great use of your sparkling personality. Creative ideas in planning. Bravo!"

I was assigned to teach English in Kralupy nad Vlatava, which means Kralupy on the Vlatava River, in a school called the Dvorákovo Gymnasium. The Peace Corps set up an initial visit for all the volunteers to their sites, so off I went to check out my home for the next two years.

Kralupy is a city of 20,000 people located exactly twenty-eight minutes north of Prague, by train. Its only claim to fame is that Dvorák's birthplace is only a half hour's walk away along the polluted Vlatava River—hence the name of the school where I would teach. Kralupy is a backwater town with countless smokestacks, chemical factories, oil refineries, and grim concrete apartment houses built by the communists. There are days in the winter when the children are made to stay indoors because the air is so polluted. It has two run-down churches, but when I asked what religions were practiced in these churches, the answer was, "We're atheists."

Kralupy did produce a Nobel prize-winning poet, Jaroslav Seifert, who wrote: "Kralupy is not a beautiful town and never was: it's a town of smoke stacks like phantom trees, without branches, without leaves, without blossoms, without bees."

The Americans bombed Kralupy heavily at the end of the Second World War because Hitler was getting his oil there. But we weren't quite on target. So we leveled much of the town. I had soon dubbed Kralupy, "Crappy Kralupy."

On my first visit, I was to be met by the school principal and the Czech English teacher, but when I arrived, there was no sign of either of them. There was no message explaining their absence. I should have seen it as a sign of things to come. Instead, the 20-year-old janitor took me under his wing on this two-day visit and showed me around the town and school. He spoke English. Another sign. If the janitors were already speaking English, why did they need Peace Corps volunteers to teach?

When the volunteers returned to Podebrady from their new teaching assignments, we had a two-hour debriefing session. Our leader asked, "Who wants to start?"

I jumped up and said, "I think we should start at the bottom and work our way up, so that means I go first." I held up a picture of Dvorák with wild hair and a mad look in his eye and said, "This is how I'll look at the end of two years."

On the other hand, I reasoned with myself, I could have ended up in Ghana living in a grass hut with a snake. Kralupy was only a 28-minute, 25-cent train ride from Prague where I had spent the last weekend at the Czech Tennis Open watching Boris Becker and John McEnroe. I had a pedicure (75 cents), manicure (50 cents), and facial (1 dollar). I attended a play by Václav Havel, the playwright president. (One volunteer joked: "Most Peace Corps volunteers go home with bad teeth and malaria, but Dicky will go home with a pedikura, manikura, and kosmetika!") There were four McDonald's in Prague, so help was close by.

I ventured forth to teach in crappy Kralupy.

But it got much worse. For one, I didn't feel at all useful. There were excellent English teachers already at the Dvořák Gymnasium and many of the students spoke good English. I felt like I was just cheap labor assigned the dirty work. During a staff meeting in the teachers' lounge, the principal insisted I stay out, as if I were not part of the staff. Another time, a teacher handed me a stack of her papers to grade. I did it, but the next time she gave me a stack, I said, "Listen, don't you think you should do this? They are your students and you need to know how they are progressing in your class." She wouldn't have any of it and I graded the next stack. It costs the Peace Corps about $40,000 to have a volunteer in position. How was I making that investment worthwhile? Other volunteers in Group V were asking the same questions. Many felt that we were no longer needed in the Czech Republic but that the Peace Corps bureaucracy just kept rolling along without evaluating its usefulness.

But the worst part of life in Kralupy was how I began to doubt myself. A very strange thing can happen to you when you've been out of your culture for a while, especially if you're thrust into a culture that's been under communism for fifty years. The communists repressed every spontaneous emotion. Fear was the overriding presence. If I greeted people on the street with a typical American hello, they would be astonished, and then bewildered, then point out to their friend that the "foreigner" just spoke, and finally laugh at you.

I stopped greeting people, even though it is my nature.

I tried to remind myself of who I am, that I had another life in America with friends, family, and connections. But slowly and imperceptibly this feeling eroded. I was only one person and they were many. I lost confidence in myself. I was an outsider. It was very hard to put my finger on exactly what was going on with my psyche. I asked myself why I was so uncomfortable. I began to think there was something wrong with me. And the downward spiral began. My confidence evaporated.

This loss of confidence is what happened to Susan, a bright and enthusiastic young volunteer, who had dreamed about the Peace Corps for as long as she could remember. She was working alone in a small village. When she started to doubt herself, she called the Prague office for assurance that what she was feeling was normal. She got nothing back. She needed to be visited or to be called in for a few days in Prague. She needed validation. When no help came, she went home. The pain of isolation was too much.

Another great volunteer who took Early Termination around this time was Dick, a man in his 50's. He was a former principal and superintendent in California, the father of seven children. He sold his home and car at a loss of $30,000 because he was so determined to join the Peace Corps. He had major concerns about his living conditions and teaching position in Pilsen, the Czech town famous for its beer. While other English teachers not from the Peace Corps were living in decent apartments, he was living in a dump. He called Prague: "I need a bed, some chairs, and a table."

"No problem," they said, but the furniture never came. On top of that, he was not given enough hours of work. Here he was in Pilsen, having made quite a sacrifice, and he felt practically useless. No one responded to his many pleas for help. At his stage in life he would not tolerate being treated unjustly or indifferently, so he simply said, "I'm not taking this crap," and took Early Termination instead.

These volunteers who took Early Termination were not

wimps. They were not babies who needed to be coddled. They were strong, dedicated people who wanted to do their part as Americans. Seeing these two admirable people head home added to my despair. I contemplated ET myself. I didn't think I could go on feeling so alienated.

Instead, I got permission to go to Germany to visit my friends in Butzbach. There were still many there, although it had been four years since I had last taught on the army base there. Within a half-hour of being with them I could feel my psyche start to return to normal. I received validation of who I was. It was like a miracle. As I contemplated returning to Kralupy, I got mad. It was Kralupy that had done this to me, made me feel so useless! This time I would hang onto my sense of self despite the conditions in Kralupy and at the Dvořák Gymnasium. I was a Peace Corps volunteer living out JFK's vision. I had been chosen because I could think on my feet, call on all my talents, and that was what I was going to do. I had done it in Karlovy Vary and I could do it again.

I ripped into my first class: "Let me tell you something, boys and girls. I don't like your town, Kralupy. Do you know how dead it is? It is just like living in a cemetery." At this point I held up a picture of Arlington Cemetery. "I don't like living in a cemetery. I don't like living with dead people."

They looked at me blankly, but I was not finished. "Yes! Look at your faces. They are dead. Hello! Is anybody home?"

I was on a rip, but I felt alive and sure of myself again. I began speaking to people I passed on the street, but it was not the wimpy "hello" I had been laughed at for before. Now I said, "Good morning, corpse. Going to your coffin?"

I sent a letter to the Prague office decrying their treatment of Susan which resulted in her ET. I sent another letter to all my fellow Peace Corps volunteers in Group V describing my "new philosophy for surviving in the Czech Republic." I told them how mad I was and how I planned to fight back.

I concluded my letter by saying, "I am not a ranting fool. I have never been so mentally healthy since our plane put down in Prague, and I will fight with all my might to stay this way. End of sermon."

This was my state of mind when the Dvořák Gymnasium celebrated its 70th birthday. It was a big deal with music and speeches, and the Peace Corps director and his assistant were invited to attend. Looking back, I wonder if part of the reason they came was because they had caught wind of my "sermon" to the other volunteers about survival. Another volunteer, Bob, pointed out that I was the only volunteer visited by the director. And it was at this celebration that the ball started rolling toward my own ET.

After the celebration I greeted a fellow teacher in the German language. This teacher was comfortable speaking German and so was I. The director heard me and was angry. "Why are you speaking German? Why are you using German as a crutch? How can you relate to these people unless you speak Czech?"

I should have said: I can relate splendidly with the Czech people in German, English, and a smattering of Czech, a language I seem unable to learn. German is a common language here because this country had been occupied by the Germans. A part of it once actually belonged to Germany, and the people were forced to speak German for many years. One of the principles of the Peace Corps is that volunteers draw on every skill they have in order to make their job work. If it meant speaking in tongues, I would have tried that, too.

I could have also pointed out that the director himself spoke little Czech and was accompanied everywhere he went by a translator. But I didn't.

Instead, I was intimidated by him, an authority figure, and simply apologized.

Then I mistakenly mentioned that I had been on a one-day tour to Vienna.

Crime #2! Now he was furious. "I could have you on the next plane to America for that. How many times do we have to tell you

150

that you are not to go out of the country without permission?" I understand the Peace Corps's reasoning. If an emergency situation developed, they have to know where you are. I did try to call the Prague office to tell them about the trip to Vienna but didn't get through. But he wasn't finished yet. "You may not use Kralupy as a jumping off point to visit the West!" The fact was that I was on a Czech tour with 46 other Czechs, I was invited by one of my Czech students, only Czech was spoken, and we were back in the Czech Republic by evening. It would be the same as if I had spent the day in Prague, according to my thinking. But he was not mollified. "You must relate to the Czech people."

When I returned to my apartment after the celebration, I felt like I had been assaulted. This man didn't even know me. He didn't know my rich background, what a great teacher I am, that my classroom was a thing of beauty, that I related splendidly with my Czech friends. I had so much to offer. Instead of honoring that, he chastised me. I now stood where Susan and Dick had stood: unsupported and unheard. And I was mad at myself that I had not stood up to this man, not defended myself.

That weekend I had planned a trip to Karlovy Vary where I had taught in 1990-1991. I was welcomed back like a heroine. "You must come back to teach here, Dicky!" they urged. "We will do everything for you! What do you want? It's yours!" Here was affirmation. They offered me a job, but I said no. I thought of JFK. I had to see my commitment with the Peace Corps through in Kralupy.

And then fate intervened. I had been sending e-mails to my brother in California through a friend in Kralupy. After the run-in with the country director, I had sent my friend a long letter full of invective against the Peace Corps: how I wished they would fire me because I didn't have the nerve to quit, how I thought my boss was like the Gestapo, how I planned to go to Budapest with a friend for Christmas even though it was against Peace Corps policy.

My friend sent this harangue to my boss in Prague by mistake. Within minutes of my friend confessing his error, I realized that my tenure with the Peace Corps was over. There was no way I could stay now.

The next 18 hours were surreal. I packed up my apartment. I didn't want to make any explanations so I went to work and taught four classes, dashing to the bank on a free period to close my account. I fired off a final e-mail to my boss: "Since you have seen fit to read my innermost thoughts, addressed to my brother, I resign from the Peace Corps as of this date." The moment school let out, I headed to the train for Prague. That night I met an American friend and we boarded a train for Budapest. I was no longer a Peace Corps volunteer.

Was my behavior immature? Probably. Did I react too quickly instead of talking the problems out? Probably. But I came under attack when I was very vulnerable. My only thought was to escape to where I could get my identity back.

This, of course, was not the way to resign from the Peace Corps. A flurry of e-mails began to hit cyberspace. International crisis. The country director in Prague wrote the following to my brother in Los Angeles:

> i am forced to treat [Dicky] as a 'missing person' according to the regulations of the Peace Corps. until she actually comes to prague and officially checks out, in person, we cannot consider her as 'resigned.' she is in possession of an official no-fee usg passport, & a peace corps-procured tax-free work permit for the czech republic. furthermore, she must sign a number of documents and do her final medical check. all of this must be completed before her resignation is official. until then, she is absent without leave.
>
> if we cannot get positive confirmation of her location VERY SOON, i will have to put out a cable to all US embassies in the region, to immigration in

all the neighboring countries, and all other US government immigration posts and cooperating foreign agencies to find her. if she might be in trouble, I would want to do this right away. if she is not, we need to have contact with her. otherwise, it could be quite embarrassing for her when she is finally located [*sic*].

I was AWOL! He was putting out an APB. I wondered if he called in Interpol.

But I never showed up at the Prague office in person. I was not about to be yanked around by these bureaucrats. I asked a fellow volunteer to return my medical kit and language books to the Peace Corps office. I mailed my special Peace Corps passport directly back to Washington, D.C. I wrote letters to the remaining members of Group V explaining what I was doing. I mailed a two-page list of all the events in which I had participated in Kralupy September 18, 1993 to December 12, 1993 so I could never be accused of being a slacker.

I was immediately welcomed back to Karlovy Vary where I started right in teaching at the School for Travel Trade and the School of Economics. I had no intention of returning to America. I still believed I had something to offer the Czech Republic, even without the Peace Corps.

On one of my first days back in Karlovy Vary, this sense that I had something to offer was affirmed. I was walking down a street when a young man ran up to me. He was pale and breathless. He stammered, "Mrs. Jensen, is that really you? I can't believe. I look out window and say is that Mrs. Jensen? I see you walk. I quickly dress and run. I think I dream."

I had given this young man, Pavel, and his friend, Robert, the opportunity to give four concerts of Beatles songs three years earlier. He had never forgotten that experience. I was worthwhile.

My attempt to honor JFK had ended badly, but I decided he

would accept my work in Karlovy Vary as sufficient homage. And, as President Bush said at the end of his tenure as president, "It was a helluva ride!"

eighteen

Taking Advantage of Friends and Relatives: Europe

I met Pedro Urbina at my sister Beba Frey's winery. Each school year, Beba has a young, future winemaker live with her. She's had students from Russia, Sweden, Italy, Germany, and Spain. (With ten of her children, their spouses, and 29 grandchildren all living on the property, what's one more?) That's how Pedro Urbina from Logroño, Spain, came to live with her for a year. Pedro and his family own a winery in the La Rioja district of Spain, famous for red wines. While Pedro studied wine making at the Frey winery, Beba fed him, helped him improve his English, and was his surrogate mother. I was in Spain to see the Guggenheim Museum in Bilbao when I noticed that Logroño was only a half-inch to the south on the map. Payback time. Without hesitation, I wrote to Pedro's family, introduced myself as Dr. Frey's sister, and asked if I might come for a short visit. The answer was never in doubt.

I spent five glorious days with Catalina and Pedro Urbina Sr., Pedro's parents. I saw every cathedral, vineyard, village, and bodega within fifty miles of the Urbina's home. I saw Spain as no tourist sees it. On the way, I also picked up a healthier attitude towards wine—it's your friend, not your enemy. Embrace it. You're not going to become an alcoholic; it's part of the meal. As you enjoy salad with each meal so you enjoy wine with each meal. That includes lunch.

The Urbinas lived in the center of Logroño. Over three days, Catalina and I explored the Old City, Parliament, the library, the post office, monasteries, convents, and parks. I stopped at the tourist office where I picked up posters of grapes and vineyards to send to the Frey Winery. We revived ourselves (sometimes *before* lunch) with a stop at a *tapas* bar for white wine and mushrooms.

Pedro Sr. spent two days driving Catalina and me all over the La Rioja region. We visited the village of LaGuardia, a medieval town surrounded by an ancient wall and filled with narrow alleyways; we saw breathtaking views of the vineyards and mountain ranges; we visited two monasteries from the year 600 A.D., San Millan Yuso, meaning the monastery down the hill, and San Millan Suso, meaning the monastery up the hill; we visited the Cathedral Santo Domingo, a stopping-off place for pilgrims who are making the five hundred mile walk to Campostella, and met pilgrims from Martha's Vineyard and Ottawa, Canada; we stopped at a country fair that is now called a "tractor" fair with not a cow or bull to be seen; we ate at the famous restaurant, La Vieja Bodega, or The Old Winery, featured in the magazine *The Wine Spectator*. We were treated as very special guests because we were vintners.

The highlight of my time in Logroño was lunch at Pedro's winery, the Urbina Bodega, housed in a five-story building, complete with tasting room, laboratories, kitchens, offices, extra bedrooms, a pool table, and a library. While there, I counted thirty-five wine tanks and saw thousands of bottles of wine.

The lunch was excellent. Catalina had carefully shopped for lamb chops of just the right thickness that morning. Pedro laid a fire using grape vines to add special flavor to the lamb. He picked out four bottles of red wine, one a *Gran Reserva* from 1986, and others from 1991, 1994, and 1995. We were each given four large, gleaming wine glasses. I learned how to put my nose in the wine glass and breathe in the aroma, how to swirl the wine around, how to hold it up to the light, and how to swish that first swallow over my tongue and teeth and concentrate on the taste. This was a sacred ritual, a meditation. With the wine and lamb chops, we dined on white asparagus, olives, chorizo, and goat cheese. It was a once in a lifetime treat.

One part of every day for Catalina and Pedro, religiously set aside and inviolate, was a visit to their parents. Catalina's mother was 88 and had suffered two strokes; she lived in a *residencia* or nursing home. As soon as Catalina walked into her mother's room she kissed her profusely all over her face. She adjusted her mother's dress and sweater to make sure she looked just right. She wheeled her up and down the halls, up the elevator, and out on the balcony for a view of the surrounding mountains. She kept up a steady conversation with her, patting her hand as she talked. There was absolutely no response from the mother that I could see, but Catalina said that her mother knew she was there.

In the meantime, Pedro Sr. was spending two hours with his aging parents, watching the news with them, getting his father into his pajamas, and tucking them both into bed. The routine never varied. With a pang of guilt, I thought of my mother living in her own residencia, Walnut Manor in Anaheim, California, and tried to remember the last time I visited her.

All too soon, my days in Logroño were over and I was on my way back to Bilbao and other points in Europe. I had had five wonderful days, saved piles of money on lodging, and got to know two warm and wonderful people. They were happy to do something for Beba's sister since Beba had done so much for their son. They said I was welcome back anytime.

I had another fabulous European adventure by seeking out my friend, Chris Skalaski in Poland. I met Chris during my aborted attempt at settling down in Michigan. For the six weeks I was there, I taught an English as a Second Language class in the evening to 14 students, and Chris was one of them. As is my practice, I take down addresses of people whom I think I might be able to find down the road. This one paid off big time.

Going to Poland at that time, 1989, without contacts, would have been a disaster. Very few people spoke English. The society was not geared to help tourists. It was almost impossible to get train information, find a hotel, or buy a meal. But then, I believe in playing it risky.

I arrived in Krakow at 7:30 one evening. I asked a taxi driver to take me to Chris's house, and through an interpreter I understood that his address was an hour outside of Krakow. The only two English words the taxi driver could speak were "No problem." The more he said them the more nervous I got. I found myself driving out in the boonies of Poland with a taxi driver who couldn't speak English and an address scribbled down two months earlier in Michigan, now a universe away.

After forty-five minutes of driving, I could feel the onset of a major anxiety attack. The driver stopped at least three times to talk to people and study the address again. I kept shrugging my shoulders at him, and he kept saying, "No problem."

I wondered what had possibly possessed me to want to go to Poland.

Finally he stopped in front of an ugly, concrete house and said, "*Deutsche Mark?*"

Oh no, you don't, I thought. You're not going to dump me here. I made him get out of the cab and try to rouse someone in the house. No doorbell, of course. No lights on. We went around the back where chickens were scratching and a dog was barking. A lady appeared on the balcony, and after about thirty long seconds, she broke out into a big smile and waved at me.

Saved.

We were at the Skalaski residence. I wasn't sure what to pay the driver in zlotys so decided to pay him in American money. I was hoping that a $20 bill would be about right for over an hour's drive at night. When I handed it to him, he looked at me as if I had given him the Island of Manhattan. Later I found out I overpaid him by $15, but President Bush, senior, had just promised the Poles a hundred million dollars so I considered this a first payment. Then my student, Chris, appeared and from then on all went wonderfully.

Chris took three days off from work. The Poles are so hospitable, it's embarrassing. One day Chris drove me to Auschwitz, the terrible concentration camp, a two-hour trip through the Polish countryside. Farmers were cutting hay with scythes, women were bundling it up and building haystacks, and horses were pulling wooden wagons.

Auschwitz was a very sobering experience. I walked through barracks piled high with thousands of pairs of shoes, toothbrushes, caps, pants, and skirts. A mile up the road was the sister camp, Birkenau. On this little spot of land four million people were killed. The Polish government keeps these camps open and doesn't charge admission so that these crimes will never be forgotten.

Another day Chris drove me to the city of Krakow where we had an all day walking tour. At the outdoor market I was able to buy many gifts for my son-in-law who is of Polish descent. His surname was Khouharsky, but when his grandfather immigrated to America, he had it changed to Cook. I had with me a picture of my daughter, her husband, David, and their new son, Lowell. I showed this picture to everyone and explained the reason I came to Poland was because of this family. When I pointed to myself and said, "*Amerikaner*," they would point to themselves and say, "Detroit" or "Chicago" or "New Jersey." I think every Pole has a relative in America.

The most striking condition about Poland was the long lines of people who had to wait interminably for everything in near-empty stores. One night, my friend needed a piece of butter so I got on the line in a dreary store where each customer had to be waited on individually by a tired looking woman in a dirty apron. All they had to sell was butter and small bottles of what looked like separated milk. I was the thirtieth person on this line. In another store, I counted fifty people in a meat line. When they were finally served they got about a pound of what looked like chopped liver. Who'd want it? The grocery stores had only jars of jam, hundreds of plastic sieves, bread, and small paint brushes. Now I ask you? And if you bought six rolls or a load of bread, they just handed it to you with no bag. I stuffed them into my raincoat pocket.

The clothing stores were just as bad. I went into one where

there were about six skirts—all ugly—twelve jackets, three pocket-books. And God forbid if I touched anything. I had to ask the tired clerk who was wearing slippers if I could look at an item. As I looked the item over, she waited while I made up my mind. In the meantime all the other customers waited for their chance to look at one of the drab skirts.

I remember when I returned to Frankfurt, I was struck dumb by the amount of sausages, pastries, and fruits being sold in the train station. And nobody waiting in line. After a few weeks in Poland, everything in the Western world was a shock.

But I was a guest at Chris's house and was saved from most of the realities of Polish life in 1989. His mother served each meal to me on a tray in the living room except the three o'clock meal which was the big one of the day. We had that when the father came home from the factory. I always had a platter of sliced tomatoes and cucumbers with raw onions and parsley sprinkled on top, fresh bread, a glass of tea, boiled eggs, ham, and cheese. Thank goodness Chris lived on a farm because all the food was right there. Rows of peppers, cabbages, beets, onions, potatoes, and watermelons. The father hunted wild pig and deer so we had that on several occasions. I was not allowed to do one stitch of work. Even suggesting that I help with the dishes brought a great cry of protest, so I finally decided to settle in and enjoy the room service.

On the third day of Chris's holiday, he drove me to Czechtohova to see The Black Madonna, a religious icon which every Catholic Pole wants to visit. She was unveiled every morning at 6. Chris's mother knocked at my door at 3 a.m. She gave me a bag of ham sandwiches, and we tore through the Polish countryside for two and a half hours to see the unveiling in the cathedral. We got there two minutes ahead of time and already the church was packed and we had to stand. I really couldn't see what was so great about The Black Madonna, but then I'm neither Polish nor Catholic. On the way home we stopped at several markets. One person, usually an older woman, would be selling one small bouquet of flowers.

Another one would be selling three clusters of garlic or two bunches of beets. Another woman was hoping to sell five sausages or one skirt or two pair of underwear or seven onions. You had to see it to believe it. Horse-drawn wooden wagons were piled high with potatoes. I felt like I was living in a time warp.

I learned that, as an American, I am so rich financially that it absolutely boggles my mind. I met a lovely teacher on a train and found out that her salary is $7 a month. Read that again. That is the truth. I had to tell her that I make that every twenty minutes. She just leaned back in her seat with this incredulous look on her face.

I had a bowl of potato soup one day and it cost one penny. So I thought, what the heck, and I tipped the waitress another penny, a 100% tip. The eight-hour train ride from Krakow to East Germany cost forty cents. A city bus ride cost one-fourth of a penny. My last hostel cost thirty-five cents. There were eight of us in the room but it was clean and comfortable.

Some days I would walk down the country road and watch the farmers at work. I'd call out *"Dzien Dobry,"* hello. Most of them stared back at me as if they couldn't believe their eyes. Did I fall off another planet? I had Chris write me a note in Polish which I gave to the people I met: "My name is Virginia Jensen. I come from America. My middle daughter is married to a Polish American so I have come to Poland to learn more about your country." One lady farmer invited me into her house and thrust a big bouquet of flowers upon me. Another couple—both with all their teeth missing—gave me a ride in their wooden wagon drawn by two horses. They kept turning around and staring at me and whispering between themselves. They couldn't take their eyes off my beautiful white teeth. I followed another woman and her teenage daughter around their fields. They kept giggling at me. This woman had three teeth. I stayed with the Skalaski family for eight fabulous days. Then Chris put me on a train headed for Warsaw. I walked through the *Alte Stadt* (Old City) which had been completely rebuilt since the war. I visited Marie Sklodoska Curie's Museum, the Presidential

Palace, the American Embassy, and the Botanical Garden. The price for a room at the Grand Hotel was $66 American dollars. Instead I rented a family's front room for $1.50. It was on the fourth floor of a dingy, concrete building with dog shit in the hallway, and many children and dogs in the apartment, but the couch was clean so I slept like a baby.

From Krakow, I went to Lublin to track down the grandmother of my nephew's wife—no connection is too distant to track. There wasn't a room to be had in Lublin except for one night in a rundown hotel. I could only stay for one night because they were going to clean the hotel and were closing it down for three days. At the height of the tourist season? Why don't they clean it in February? And why do you have to close down a hotel to clean it? The receptionist in the hotel was very nicely dressed. We started up a conversation which led to talking about her sister who lived in California. The receptionist's name was Grazyna. I asked Grazyna if she didn't have a friend who would like to rent me a room for a few days. She said, "I tinking. I tink maybe you come my house."

I whispered, "I'll pay you in American dollars." I was in. So I stayed with Grazyna for the next five nights and slept on the living-room couch. She had waited fifteen years to get this apartment. Her 78-year-old father lived with her, and he had had two heart attacks and was now into Alzheimer's. When we came home each night she would cross herself and ask, "What I find?" Twice we found him sprawled out on the floor staring at the ceiling. Who knows how long he'd been there?

Grazyna was essential in helping me find my nephew's Polish wife's family. It took two buses and asking questions of many people (all in Polish, of course) to find this little house on a little side street, UL. Kowicka. I couldn't have done it without Grazyna.

When we finally found the house, Maria Sagan, a short, plump 76-year-old woman greeted us at the door. When she heard that I was bringing greetings from her grandchild in America whom she hadn't seen in twelve years, she kissed me again and again and ushered us into her living room. It was arranged that I would come back in a few hours when her daughter, Gregenna, and husband, Tadeosh, who both spoke English, would be home.

I returned on time with a bottle of Vodka (two American dollars) and a bottle of whiskey (another two dollars). I bought the liquor in a special store where they only accept American dollars. Maria, who couldn't speak English, sat me in front of the TV. I waited for an hour for the daughter and husband to return. Finally, at 6:30 the grandmother brought me a plate of seven boiled potatoes and a piece of meat. I wondered what happened to the daughter. I thought we were to have dinner together. I didn't understand what was going on; and not being able to communicate (a major handicap), I went ahead and ate the dinner by myself. Finally after another hour of waiting, I got very uneasy and decided I would go back to Grazyna's house. I gave the grandmother the whiskey and vodka and indicated I was leaving. She got very agitated. "No, lady, no lady. Please, lady." She ushered me upstairs and quickly opened up a couch into a bed, put on a sheet and quilt as she kept saying, "Please, lady." I was getting frustrated and angry. I didn't understand what was happening. I felt trapped in this house with a woman I could not communicate with. So I thought, well, I'll open up the bottle of whiskey I brought as a present and give myself a shot. Then I got out a piece of paper and started to write down the names of American songs in an attempt to hold onto my sanity. Finally at 10 o'clock the rest of the Sagan family arrived. They spoke English. What a relief to be able to communicate again.

The next day, the Sagans took me to their farm, 40 kilometers away. There I met their 23-year-old nephew, Jakub, who spoke excellent English. He considered me his complete responsibility and became my constant guide and interpreter. He invited me to stay in his tenth floor apartment, and because I didn't want to wear out my welcome with Grazyna or Maria Sagan, I agreed. Do you for one minute think I would go up a 20-year-old Polish elevator? No way. Does anyone for a minute believe that if you pushed the emergency button when the elevator got stuck that someone would come? Ridiculous thought. I considered it a delight to walk up the ten flights of stairs.

Jakub took at least one hundred pictures of me. Photography is his hobby but one hundred pictures? There is Dicky in front of every building in Lublin. Oh, there is Dicky in front of six different haystacks. Oh, there she is walking down twelve different streets.

He took me to his parents' home. His father is a judge and his mother a gynecologist. She came home from the hospital two hours early because an American visitor was there. We ate from the best china on a linen tablecloth. Jakub did all the talking for me as we dined on four courses.

Finally he accompanied me on the five-hour train trip back to Krakow. He wanted to make sure I would get on the right train heading to Frankfurt.

If not for Chris Skalaski and Jakub Sagan, this trip to Poland would have been just about impossible. With their help, Poland opened up to me. And there are more Chrises and Jakubs out there. My fat, black address book is filled with names and addresses of people who have said, "Come visit me if you are ever in my city." My traveling life is all about following up on these invitations. It has worked for 18 years, and I have more years in me.

nineteen

America the Beautiful

I t was a Eureka! moment. I was traveling across America in a minivan with my sister and brother-in-law and we had just pulled into Yellowstone National Park. Rather than eating groceries out of the back of the van on paper plates, we decided to treat ourselves to dinner in a park restaurant. Never has eating in a restaurant been so good for me.

The hostess who escorted us to our table was—to use a word I detest—elderly.

"Hmmm," I thought, "I wonder how she managed to get hired."

Then the waitress appeared. Also elderly.

My curiosity was definitely aroused, and I sensed I was on the verge of some very important information.

On the way out of the restaurant I casually asked our hostess, "Is it difficult to get a job here? I would certainly be interested in working in such a unique environment."

"Oh, no. They're always looking for good help."

"And what about living quarters? Do they give you housing?"

"Oh, definitely. We live in a dormitory right near here, and we eat in the employee dining room."

That was all I needed to hear. Cheap food and housing while I got paid to live in some of the most beautiful places in America, talking to tourists from all over the country and all over the world. My idea of perfect. And there are 87 national parks from the Everglades in Florida to the Grand Canyon in Arizona to Denali in Alaska. This definitely needed looking into.

So when I was saturated with looking at cathedrals and museums and sharing bedrooms with fellow travelers in other countries, I decided to look into the national parks. I got busy on the Internet. Fifty pages spewed out: types of jobs, rates of pay, living conditions, rent rates, recreational opportunities, length of jobs, transportation, applications, and instructions on how to apply. All very straightforward. It didn't take me long to spot that the monthly rent for an employee at the Grand Canyon National Park was $64.

I was cat-sitting in New York City when I put my application in the mail. That was Monday. On Friday afternoon, the telephone rang. It was the Human Resources Office at the Grand Canyon asking me how soon I could come out.

"Why, eh, uh, I'll be there next week."

The National Parks are desperate for good employees. By "good," I mean those who don't call in sick when they really have a hangover, those who don't show up late because "the alarm didn't go off," those who don't ask for extra days off, and those who don't up and leave with no notice when they get tired of the job. The parks want employees who simply show up on time, give 100% to the employer, and stay till the end of their contract. Isn't that what an employee is supposed to do?

I flew to Las Vegas and then caught the Scenic Airways Tour plane to the Grand Canyon which offered a breathtaking view of the canyon, my future home for five months. When I landed at Grand Canyon Village, I called the Human Resources Office to announce my arrival, and they sent out a cab to pick me up. It took three hours to be tested for drugs, have my picture taken for my ID, have benefits explained, be issued bedding and towels, and be transported to Colter Hall, a women's dormitory which sits fifty feet from the rim of the canyon, the same distance as the El Tovar Hotel where rooms start at $125 per night.

My room was large, sunny, and overlooked the Grand Canyon

train station. Every day at 12:15 the train whistle announced the arrival of the train from Williams, Arizona, seventy-five miles to the south. My roommate was a Navajo woman, Tammy Blackwater.

My job? I was assigned to the Curio Shop as a sales clerk in the El Tovar Hotel, the oldest and most elegant hotel on the south rim of the Grand Canyon. We called it the "El Ta-Ta." My uniform was khaki pants and a denim shirt. I learned how to fold T-shirts properly, the most boring part of the job; how to wrap glass cacti so they would arrive in some foreign country in one piece; how to spot a shoplifter (very easily—the guilty looks are so obvious); how to balance out the cash drawer at the end of a shift; and most importantly, how to communicate and enjoy the company of tourists from around the world.

At the Grand Canyon, the drudgery of day to day life was transformed. Need to go to the post office? Walk half-an-hour along the rim of the Canyon, through a lovely forest and see lots of wildlife. Time to fix lunch? Eat at the Yavapai Lodge or Maswik Lodge for 50% off the menu prices, a privilege accorded employees. There was a well-stocked library, a free employee shuttle to Flagstaff every other week, and a recreation building.

At the end of five months, I had a healthy bank account, had experienced one of the Seven Wonders of the World, had learned about the life of Native Americans, and could fold a T-shirt in 20 seconds. Who could ask for anything more?

I was hooked on the national park scene.

Why not go to Alaska next? The Land of the Midnight Sun, the Iditerod, Robert Service and his poetry. The 49th State would surely be good for some new experiences.

I went back to the Internet, filled out another application and sat back and waited. It didn't take long. Before the week was out, management at Denali National Park called asking me to come to work.

This time I applied for a job at the front desk. This meant learning how to operate a computer—I who had always used a manual typewriter using a handheld rubber eraser and carbon paper to make extra copies. All these items can now be seen in a museum of ancient history.

Making reservations on the computer was by no means a straightforward job. For example, someone would call up to reserve two nights for two people. The interrogation begins. Are you with children or without? Did you want rafting tickets and, if so, on what trip and are the children over 16 years of age? Oh, you need a handicapped room or tickets for the nightly show, *Cabin Nite*? Yes, we can give you a river-view room, but that has a different price than the rooms that look at the parking lot. And on and on into every detail of a person's life.

The upside of my job on the front desk was that I could take advantage of freebies. The people on the front desk have a great influence on steering the guests to the many commercial attractions the park has to offer. But in order to recommend the horseback riding or the rafting, we have to have experienced it. So I signed up for the free helicopter ride that landed on two glaciers; an airplane ride that circled Mt. McKinley; a two-hour horseback ride over streams and forests (which I never recommended because the wear and tear on my back and butt were not worth it); and a two-hour rafting trip down the Nenana River.

But the computer was still a mystery. I persevered for two solid weeks. Here and there, I could glimpse a dull light at the end of a long tunnel, but my future on the front desk certainly didn't look bright.

Then salvation came in the form of a kindly pat on my arm and the words from my supervisor, "Dicky, could I speak with you for a moment?" as she led me to her office. "The General Manager needs someone to take charge of the ice-cream stand and wonders if you would like to be that person. Would you possibly consider doing that instead of working the front desk?"

Would I! I definitely can distinguish between vanilla, chocolate, and strawberry ice cream.

"I would *love* that job!" I know I sounded too anxious and too relieved, but no matter, I was finished with the computer chaos and on to something more civilized.

My first challenge was to come up with a fun uniform that would attract the tourists to the ice-cream stand. This I could handle. In one of the gift shops I found a bright red apron covered with images of black moose and a tall chef's hat to match. Along with black slacks, a white shirt, earrings, and bright red Tommy Hilfiger running shoes, I was transformed into The Ice-Cream Lady.

I quickly added two more jobs to my repertoire: breakfast hostess and "room stripper." Working in the beautiful lodge rooms of McKinley Village, I stripped guestrooms of sheets, towels, trash, and coffee cups. It was like going to a fitness center: bend, stretch, lift, throw, pull, and off to the next room. I was called the best stripper in town.

Fortunately, my father had instilled a work ethic in his children that all work is honorable. Even pulling bags of dirty sheets and trash down the hall could be a badge of honor. And I did this noble work while looking at the beautiful Nenana River just outside the guestroom windows. I kept my body active and my mind sharp. I earned money and lived in the majestic state of Alaska.

At this park, I was assigned a room in a trailer. That was a first. We employees quickly referred to our trailer complex as Trailer Trash Village. The bathrooms and showers were a three-minute walk from the trailers, but since it stayed light all night, that two a.m. trek to the bathroom, affectionately named The Petri Dish, was actually pleasant. I decorated the walkway along our trailers with plants I "borrowed" from the dining room. Every whiskey, vodka, gin, and beer bottle became a vase in which I put daisies, heather, pine branches, or whatever happened to be in bloom.

On my days off, I was entitled to free bus rides into Denali National Park. I always ordered a bag lunch the night before from the employee dining room and then took the all-day, 90-mile ride into the park. Before the summer was over, I had seen innumerable

169

bears with their cubs, moose, elk, wolves, beaver, martens, and eagles. And, of course, majestic Mount McKinley in all her glory. Only 25% of tourists who visit Denali get to view Mt. McKinley because she is so often shrouded in clouds. But if you live in her neighborhood for four months, you are guaranteed to see her many times.

The summer I worked in Denali, 2001, was the 50th Anniversary of Barbara and Bradford Washburn's historic climb up the west buttress of Mt. McKinley. In 1947, Barbara was the first woman to climb Mt. McKinley. When she was asked by reporters what her thoughts were when she got to the top she replied, "I wished I were home [in Boston] with my three babies." Her only training to prepare for this climb was "pushing a baby carriage." Brad was responsible for making the first full map of McKinley (it is still in use), and he led the first expedition up the west buttress, which is the most commonly used route to this day. Barbara, aged 88, and Brad, aged 91, flew from Boston to Alaska to present two slide lectures to celebrate their contributions to McKinley and mountaineering history. It was Standing Room Only.

I had met the Washburn's before because they spent part of their summers on Squam Lake in New Hampshire as I did, and I was thrilled to renew the friendship. I made the dumb mistake of asking Barbara, "And who helped you out from Boston on the plane?" She looked at me incredulously. "No one helped us out. We got on the plane and here we are." These two active, alive people are my heroes. They proved, as I was trying to, that you could reach a ripe old age being active and alive all the way.

I had now worked two short-term jobs in magnificent settings, the Grand Canyon and Denali. I wasn't ready to stop. I began my search for job #3 in yet another magnificent setting. It practically fell into my lap.

Every summer the ski resorts of Park City and Deer Valley in Utah conduct a job fair at Denali to recruit employees for their winter season. Denali and much of Alaska is frozen shut during the

170

winter so all of the people working the summer season need jobs for the winter. More importantly, Park City and Deer Valley were going to be the settings of the 2002 Winter Olympics. There was no question in my mind that I would be moving south to Utah to work and to absorb the atmosphere of the Olympics.

I had dabbled with sales, housekeeping, being a hostess and an ice-cream lady. It was time to try something new. I applied for the Entry Level Cook position. Via phone, the executive chef at Deer Valley asked if I had ever cooked professionally. "No," I had to admit, "but I raised three children over a 30-year span so I have lots of experience." That was good enough for her, and a week later I was off to the XIX Olympic Games.

I flew to Salt Lake City and then took a taxi thirty miles north to Deer Valley. The taxi driver dropped me off a little before dawn, in the cold, in front of a deserted lodge called Snow Park Lodge.

"Now what have I gotten myself into," I thought. Well, nothing to do but march forward. The automatic sliding doors opened, which I looked on as a very positive sign.

And it was warm inside, another good omen. I walked through the deserted restaurant to the kitchen. If I was going to be an entry level cook, my brilliantly logical mind told me, the kitchen would be the logical place to go. There were baskets of doughnuts, bagels and cream cheese, and hot coffee all laid out. I knew then that job #3 would be a good one.

In very quick order I had my picture taken for my ID, was issued a key to my dormitory (two bus rides and 40 minutes away), and was handed a five-piece uniform.

The uniform was not to be believed. There were black and white checked pants, a double-breasted white jacket, a white apron, a white scarf tied around my neck to catch perspiration, and the crowning glory: a tall, pleated white chef's hat. I was given my new uniform and a new identity. I was now an official cook in the number one ski resort in North America.

Cutting my first onion, it was obvious that I didn't know what

I was doing. "Put your thumb at the bottom of the blade to get better leverage." "Curl your fingers up or you'll chop one off." "No, the onion pieces have to be all the same size." I thought I knew the simple procedure of dicing an onion, but when you're working with professionals who have been to culinary school in Paris, you quickly look like an amateur.

But my outgoing personality saved me again. Rather than being a cook, I was offered the job of working on the luncheon line and serving the skiers. When I was a teacher, I had been able to organize 25 first graders into reading groups and march them off to recess and lunch at the exact ringing of a bell. I should be able to organize 25 food items and 28 garnishes, I reasoned.

So that's exactly where I ended up. Every morning my Chilean coworker and I spent two and a half hours decorating the 30-foot luncheon line with colored peppers, squash, raw carrots, leeks, and cucumbers. Or we'd have a fruit motif and do a red apple, peach, green apple, and orange combination. There were always three soups, each with its own garnish, and two chilies including our famous Deer Valley Turkey Chili which even had 2,000 Olympic pins fashioned after it. There were chicken and vegetarian enchiladas with red chili sauce or green tomatillo pepper sauce; sumptuous deli sandwiches on a choice of pita bread, sourdough, multigrain, or rye swirl; three kinds of pizza; pasta with a choice of three sauces, such as pork loin with apples, vegetable marinara, or a crab and corn sauce. At the end of the line there was the Carvery where a beautifully browned turkey breast and a New York Strip that was always pink and tender awaited the knife.

At the stroke of 11 a.m. we donned our black aprons over our white uniforms, pulled on our latex gloves, and began the mantra that would take us through the next four and a half hours: "Hello, may I help you?"

Almost all of our guests were gracious and appreciative. But there was always one each day who had to know "Do you have any pasta without the green stuff (parsley) on it?"

172

"Is the base of the enchiladas corn or wheat?"

"Are there onions in the tuna salad? I can't eat onions."

And always, when the line was longest, someone would ask, "May I taste the two chilies so I know which one I'd like?"

To myself, I'd say, "Do you mean that at this stage of your life you still haven't figured out what your tastes are?" Having been raised in the Depression where you never questioned food, where you were taught to eat everything on your plate and say thank you for the privilege of having something to eat, these questions were a source of major annoyance. But with a brilliant smile I always responded with a positive, "But, of course! You'll love tasting our chilies."

The worst customer was the American child. You could hear the whine from 40 feet away. "I want a Coke."

"No, you can't have a Coke for breakfast."

"But I want a Coke!"

Wail, wail. Did the underdeveloped dwarf no more than three years old get his Coke? Of course! The parents of this era have turned over their power to their kids. The parents look harassed and unhappy; the dwarfs call all the shots.

One very harassed mother brought a baked potato (cost: $6.25) back to our line with the distressing news, "Bobby doesn't like the way Daddy cut the potato! Could we have another one?" The $6.25 potato got tossed into the trashcan.

Me: "Here's another potato. I hope Daddy cuts it right this time."

Mother: "I hope I live long enough to see Bobby grow up."

My thinking: "Why don't you give Bobby a good smack and then everyone would be happy?"

But I come from the days when dinosaurs roamed the earth so what do I know about child rearing?

After four and a half hours of dishing out chili and enchiladas, it was time to break down the line and make room for the Seafood Buffet which followed. The seafood people had to set up

173

their lobster pots, buoys, shells, and fake fish. Our fruit and vegetable decorations had to be dismantled till the next day.

Our supervisor, trained in Paris, was very, very strict. The pizza slices had to form a circle and not be strewn about, willy-nilly. The napkin seams in the breadbaskets had to face downward. Never upwards, God forbid. Keep those soups stirred so they don't form a skin! And why did we use a back-of-the-house ladle and not a front-of-the-house ladle?

I learned the inner workings of a top-notch restaurant. It was like being part of a major theatre production. Each person chopped, shredded, grilled, fried, carved, and sliced to produce a taste experience that the guest would remember forever.

The Deer Valley resort provided excellent dormitory housing for its employees. In fact, the dorms were more like a hotel. Each room, shared by two people, came with its own bathroom, shower, and TV. The 40-minute bus ride to work was a pain, but it was free, took us through beautiful mountain scenery, and was still shorter than many "normal" people's commute to their jobs.

For the first time in then seventeen years of traveling, I did run into a dud of a roommate. I've lived with women from every country in the world, every religion, every age, and every sexual orientation. I could always get along. But here I hit a brick wall. My roommate in Deer Valley had no conception that I, too, occupied the room. I would walk in and say, "Hello, Anna." No response. I would leave and say, "I'm going to the health center now. See you later." Nothing. She had friends in to watch movies till all hours, completely oblivious that my bed was three feet from the television set and that I had to be in it at a decent hour to be ready for work the next morning.

So I put a hex on her. I reasoned, if you don't acknowledge that I exist then I won't acknowledge that you exist. When I entered our room I wouldn't say hello. When I left the room I wouldn't say good-bye. I treated her as she treated me: invisible.

The hex worked. She was gone with all her belongings a few

 174

weeks later. In her place I got a sweet woman from Chile, and all was right with the world again. So I run into a glitch now and then, but it still adds up to a magnificent life.

Of course, the high point of this job was the Olympics. And again, thanks to my Brooklyn personality, I was asked to be a server in the Press Café during the games. Right in the middle of the action. Just where I love to be. I served breakfast, lunch, and snacks to journalists from all around the world covering the events.

The Press Café was a makeshift restaurant built on a parking lot. Walls and office cubicles were installed, and large plastic tubes pumped in heat. There were computers, telephones, and television sets that received live feed from each Olympic venue. A huge rug covered the floor, and twenty circular tables each had a potted plant. My work during the Olympics was tough. First of all, I had to be at work at 6 in the morning which meant leaving my room at 4:30, riding the bus for 40 minutes and then getting dropped off *outside* the Olympic perimeter. I walked ten minutes in the dark, cold morning to the security tent to wait in line with the other employees so our bags and purses and pockets could be checked. Then it was another ten-minute walk to the restaurant. There were a few mornings when I wondered if I was going to survive the cold, the darkness, and the uphill climb.

Once I got to work, we had to move all of the food, utensils, and serving apparatuses from the regular restaurant, down an elevator, a staircase, and a long hallway to the Press Café. Only once did I consider confessing that I was 76 years old and perhaps not up to lugging heavy, hot pots of chili and soup around, but I quickly squelched that idea. I wanted the job.

Deer Valley was the venue for mogul skiing and the aerials. From the Press Café I could hear the PA on the mountainside. I could watch live feed from all the Olympic events. I saw the Australian journalist beside himself with happiness when Alisa Camplin won a gold medal in the aerials. I saw the thrill of the Czech journalist when Ales Valenta won a gold medal for doing a triple back flip with five complete twists, the first time this trick was done in an Olympic aerial competition. There was only one fan in the stands waving the Czech flag for Ales, but never mind, the Czech Republic went wild with happiness at this incredible feat.

The whole atmosphere of the Olympics was electric. Our city buses suddenly filled up with the influx of visitors. Main Street in Park City was closed off to traffic and became the place to trade pins, wear the popular Roots U.S. official beret, listen to bands and choruses and barber shop quartets, watch the Budweiser Clydesdale horses parade by, shop for Olympic souvenirs, and eat a bowl of turkey chili.

Salt Lake City was so proud that nothing went wrong. The weather was perfect. Transportation worked. Even the pairs figure-skating scandal added a bit of spice. In the small state of Utah the world came together for 17 remarkable days in friendship and sportsmanship. And Dicky was there.

I even met Penny Pack, the mother of the silver medallist in the aerials, Joe Pack. I had joined a health club near my dormitory and spent at least two hours there each day sitting in the sauna, swimming in the lap pool, rolling around on exercise balls, or relaxing in the steam room. One evening I was in the outdoor Jacuzzi, looking at the moon rising over the snow-capped mountains, a gentle snow falling on my head. A lady and her daughter got into the Jacuzzi with me. As usual, I said, "Hello! Isn't this wonderful?" A conversation ensued and before they got out, the lady said, "You should come to my house for tea sometime! I'm Penny Pack, Joe's mother. Joe is the aerialist." What a generous and unexpected invitation.

But I got nervous. I just could not work up the nerve to call this woman and say, "Remember me from the Jacuzzi? You invited me over for tea?" In the meantime I wrote a letter to my friend Toshiko Tsurumi who had been the women's ski champion of Japan in 1942. I wanted to tell her all about the Olympics. I mentioned the invitation from Penny Pack and that I didn't have the nerve to call her. I got a letter back immediately. "Dicky, call Penny Pack! This is a big opportunity!" Toshiko commanded.

I screwed up my courage and called Penny.

"I'll pick you up in the morning at the health spa!" came the friendly reply.

The next morning an SUV pulled up driven by Penny and off we went into the mountains to her beautiful house for our tea party. Penny could not have been more warm and friendly. She showed me all around her house, showed me all the trophies Joe and his brother had won over their years of skiing. When it was time to leave, she gave me a picture of Joe in the middle of one of his tricks. He had signed it. I sent it right off to Toshiko who had saved me from missing this opportunity.

And then it was over. After 17 glorious days, the high energy crowds that filled Main Street trading pins and sporting Roots berets were gone. The Clydesdale horses disappeared. The cables were cut and the TV's went blank. The last skier came down the mountain, and the Press Café was again a parking lot.

It was time to think about another national park. I had heard that Glacier National Park was the most beautiful spot in America, if not the world. I was ready to check that out.

The desperate recruiters at Glacier thought I would be a perfect assistant manager of the Swift Current Camp Store selling worms, firewood, beer, groceries, and assorted souvenirs to the campers and hikers.

I arrived in Glacier and was immediately awed by its incredible beauty. It is, without a doubt, the most spectacular park in America. I settled into a cozy, two-room cabin with a friendly roommate. I hiked through fabulous scenery, spotted lots of wildlife, and saw bear grass in bloom—this only happens every seven years. I even attended an Indian powwow where hundreds of Native Americans sang and danced dressed in feathers, moccasins, and beads.

I became good friends with the manager of the gift shop at the

Many Glacier Hotel, just ten minutes down the road from my camp store. We arranged to have the same days off. She owned a red convertible so every Wednesday and Thursday you could spot the "two old hens" flying down the road, hair blowing in the wind, just like they were in their right minds.

We explored the Blackfeet Indian Reservation in Browning. We crossed the border into Canada, just 20 miles away, and visited Ft. McCloud, the Blackfeet Indian Reservation at Flathead Lake, and the Waterton International Peace Park. We had a fascinating tour through a Hutterite Colony, ate buffalo burgers, shopped in Indian trading posts, saw herds of cattle being rounded up by cowboys on horseback, and generally loved the Big Sky country of Montana and Canada.

While my time off was superb, one aspect of my work began to annoy me. The concession company that ran the camp store seemed to be only concerned with the bottom line. My chief priority was to satisfy and take care of the needs of the campers who had traveled hundreds or thousands of miles to be with us in Glacier.

For example, our store sold one-load boxes of laundry soap for 55 cents. Everyone wanted these small boxes, but we always ran out. So the customers had to buy a huge box of laundry soap for $5. Many of them were on motorcycles and the big box was a hassle. Where would they cram a big box of soap on their bikes? I had a brilliant idea. Why not take a big box and make little plastic bags filled with soap, enough for one load? The customers would be happy, and we would make even a little more money on each box of soap.

"Can I see you in the back room, Dicky?"

Uh oh. I felt like I was being sent to the principal's office.

"What are you doing? You can't change the prices like this. The Park Service sets the prices and no mere clerk in the store can decide that the prices and packaging should be changed."

"But the guests don't want the big box," I cried in my own defense. It didn't matter. I had sinned against the hierarchy. That is a huge no-no.

At one point our store was out of ice, bottled water, power bars, and blueberry yogurt. The season is only four months long which meant that the bureaucrats had eight months to order supplies and prepare for the coming season. Was it too much to ask to have bottles of water available for the hikers who were out in the woods all day?

It was time to move on. I had spent parts of two years living and working in the most scenic spots in America. Now there were other places in the world to see.

twenty

The Agony and the Ecstasy

Dicky to foreign friend: "You have to come to America some day and visit. I'd love to take you around New York."
Foreign friend: "Oh, I'd never go to New York."
Dicky: "Why not?"
Foreign friend: "I don't want to get shot!"

heard the same dire predictions before I set off for South America. "Oh, don't go there. The people are very poor, and they'll spot you immediately as a tourist and rob you blind." Or "If you don't speak Spanish or Portugese (I don't), don't even think about going to South America. They don't speak English down there."

Both predictions turned out to be completely false. They do speak English down there, and they did spot me as a tourist but didn't rob me blind. Instead they treated me with the utmost courtesy, kindness, and friendliness.

I had met many South Americans while working at the Olympics in Utah. At least seventy of my fellow-employees hailed from Chile, Brazil, Columbia, Uruguay, and Argentina. They were the friendliest people I had ever met. They kissed me on each cheek when I arrived for work. They gently touched my arm when they spoke to me. They were helpful, laughed a lot, and worked very hard. No wonder the management went out of its way to hire people from South America.

Mateus, a twenty-three year old busboy, invited me to visit his hometown, Curitiba, two hours south of Sao Paulo, Brazil. I told him my misgivings about going to South America.

"Dicky, Curitiba is very beautiful. I will bring you a brochure."

The brochure showed a picture of the botanical gardens, an opera house, and a museum.

"Hmm, maybe this place is more civilized than I thought," I deliberated with myself. "Maybe I better give Brazil some further reflection, keep an open mind. In fact, I should find out for myself what Brazil is all about." After all, I had Mateus, an invaluable contact, who promised to help me see his beautiful country.

I decided to go to Brazil.

It turned out to be the right decision. I spent two glorious months in this lovely country being shepherded to the right hotels and sightseeing attractions by the best guide in the world and now my lifelong friend, 23-year-old Mateus. He didn't even seem aware that I could be his great-grandmother.

Mateus picked me up at the airport in his mother's car and whisked me to the Prince Eduardo VII Hotel where my reserved room on the 11th floor was waiting for me. It overlooked the central plaza, the old Cathedral, the crowds scurrying from store to store, and the price was $15 per night.

"Dicky, if you don't like this hotel, I will find you another one."

"Oh, no, Mateus, I *love* this hotel." The $15 price tag came with a buffet breakfast that consisted of four fresh fruits, three fresh juices, a variety of breads, cheeses, cakes, cookies, and hot-dogs with scrambled eggs. What was there not to like?

This particular province of Brazil is called Paraná. It was settled by German and Italian immigrants during the last century. Their influence is still greatly in evidence. So, the second week Mateus put me on a bus to Blumenau where the largest Oktoberfest outside of Munich, Germany was going to take place. Mateus gave me

182

notes in English and Portuguese he had typed up and which accompanied me on each journey.

"Bus Driver, Please be sure my American friend gets off in Blumenau. Please give her a window seat so she can see the scenery. Thank you very much for taking care of her."

The next note was for the taxi driver in Blumenau.

"Dear Taxi Driver, Please take my American friend to the Gloria Hotel where she has a reservation. Thank you very much for taking care of her."

The third note was for the receptionist at the front desk of the hotel:

"Dear Front Desk, This is my American friend, Virginia Jensen. I made a reservation for her for a week at your hotel so she could experience Oktoberfest. Enclosed is the voucher for her stay. Please help her find German restaurants and the different events connected with Oktoberfest. Thank you very much for taking care of her."

Was I well taken care of or what?

For the next week I spoke German almost exclusively. These third generation immigrants have kept their German heritage completely intact. In the nightly parades through town, the women wore dirndl dresses with aprons; the men wore lederhosen and knee-high white socks; and they hoisted their beer mugs singing "Ein Prosit, ein Prosit, Der Gemütlickkeit."

In the five huge beer halls, oompah-bands played nightly as people danced and ate *Wienerschnitzel, Rotkohl, Kartoffelbrei, Gebratene Hühner,* and so on. Was I really in Brazil or was this Munich?

Again with Mateus's help, I decided to head to Rio de Janeiro. Brazil is a country of great contrasts between the rich and the poor, and this is no more evident than in Rio. The rich live in sumptuous homes on the mountainsides overlooking the beautiful harbor. But right next to them live the poor in shantytowns called *favelas.* The biggest *favela* houses over a million poor people.

"Don't go near the *favelas*" was the most frequent admonition I heard from my friends when I told them I was planning a trip to Rio. "They are run by drug lords." "You won't come out alive." "They are very dangerous places." And on and on.

By now I take these dire predictions with a box of salt. And thank goodness I do or I would have missed a unique opportunity to see how people in *favelas* live.

A jeep tour into a *favela* was advertised in the lobby of my hotel. I immediately made my reservation. The jeep held ten of us. Our friendly female guide, Renata, immediately assured us that we had nothing to fear and that she had many friends in the *favela* whom we would meet.

The *favela* stretched up the entire side of the mountain. It was a mish-mash of shacks piled one on top of the other. There was no rhyme or reason to its layout. Electrical wires were jumbled up everywhere because the people cut into the city wires so they wouldn't have to pay electric bills. The streets were narrow, winding alleyways. It would be impossible for a stranger to find his way through this labyrinth. There were no house numbers or street names. The mail was delivered into boxes at certain locations, and the inhabitants had to go through these boxes to see if they had a letter.

Originally the houses were made out of big wooden boxes which had no windows. Now the people of Rio's *favelas* are building their homes with bricks and discarded lumber so they have windows and doors. When a child gets married an additional story is added on top since there's no room left to spread sideways.

Our first stop was at an outdoor art school where eleven- and twelve-year-old boys were being taught how to paint. The teacher hoped to steer these boys away from a life selling or taking drugs to something more constructive. We each bought an oil painting. Mine, which cost $3, was painted by Lua. For the rest of the tour Lua held my hand as we worked our way through the alleyways, stopped in pathetic, dark rooms to say hello to Renata's friends,

184

bought bottled water in the tiny, dark spaces that were the *favela* stores, and stared at the people, all of whom seemed to be happy and outgoing. Despite the extreme poverty, there was definitely a friendly, cooperative spirit in the air.

On this tour, there was nothing to be afraid of in the *favelas*. Yes, drugs control the shanty towns. The drug warlord makes all the decisions. Renata couldn't tell us who he was or where he lived; that's a closely guarded secret. And, no, I wouldn't enter a *favela* without a guide.

Brazil embodies the greatest disparity in standards of living. High above the poverty in the *favelas* stands the most recognizable symbol of Rio de Janeiro: the glistening white statue of Christ called Christus Redemptor. It stands tall astride the highest mountain and looks down on the stark contrast of lives below: shacks and mansions, the wretched and the privileged.

My trip to South America taught me not to listen to dire predictions, so I am rethinking Africa, too. It is another continent I have been afraid to visit. Who knows where my journey will take me next?

Epilogue

*"But what are you going to do
when you get too old to travel?"*

This is the inevitable question. I see it in people's faces as I describe my lifestyle.

My answer is simple. I plan never to be too old to stop traveling. I will keep putting one foot in front of the other until the Grim Reaper just takes me where I am standing. Right now, I'm way out in front of him.

I do have plan B, just in case. I can always head to my sister's winery in Redwood Valley, California. Given the crowd she's got living there now, I won't even be noticed. There are three doctors living on the property, so if I have any health issues, I'll be in the right place. I even sent her $5,000 as a "time-share" payment to ensure that I will get a bed if the need should ever arise. Living at the winery, being visited by my nieces and nephews and their numerous children, and looking at the ripening grapes and redwood groves sounds like a better solution than ending up in an old folks' home. I'm even guaranteed all the free organic wine I can drink. It sounds like a beautiful way to make my exit.

Until then, I will stay on the road. When Death comes knocking, he's going to have a heck of time finding my door.